Barnsley Gardens

At
Woodlands

The Illustrious Dream

By Clent Coker

Best Wishes
Clent Coker 2003

The Julia Company

Printed in the United States of America

Library of Congress Cataloging-in-publishing data
Coker, Clent
Barnsley Gardens at Woodlands, The Illustrious Dream

ISBN 0-9701936-0-2

Printing and graphic designs by: McStatts' Printing Co., Inc.

Edited by: Anthia McStatts

Art renderings by: A. Renee Dollar - Copyright © 2000 The Julia Publishing Co.

Photography by: Oscar Coker, Clent Coker, Alexandra Fugger, Bill Owens, Buddy Autry

Historical photographs and art renderings from the Clent Coker Collection unless otherwise noted. Copyright © 2000 by The Julia Publishing Company.

The Julia Company
3930 Spalding Drive
Atlanta, Georgia 30350

The Exotic Green Rose of Woodlands

Rosa chinesis var. Viridiflora

Dedicated To

Godfrey Barnsley
Founder of Barnsley Gardens
at
Woodlands

With tribute to my wonderful grandparents
Who first took me to the front gates of
Godfrey Barnsley's Woodlands,
and to all the Barnsleys for kindly inviting me in.

A special dedication to my wife, Laura, and our children
Who have long endured the years of research and
writing on the Barnsleys
and to my sister and brother-in-law,
Paula and Marshall Owens, who believed
in my work and spent endless hours in promoting its success.

Also to my dear friends, Gene and Barbara Martin,
of Guntersville, Alabama
Who kindly provided me a secluded home away from home
in which to write

With great appreciation to Prince Hubertus Fugger
and his wife, Alexandra,
for preserving the remainder of
Godfrey Barnsley's illustrious dream –
Barnsley Gardens at Woodlands.

TABLE OF CONTENTS

Introduction

Conclusion:

BARNSLEY GARDENS
AT WOODLANDS

INTRODUCTION

It was more than a half-century ago that I was introduced to this valuable historic treasure of antebellum America, "Barnsley Gardens at Woodlands".

Built during a time when great plantations ruled in the old South, the huge Italinate style Barnsley Manor, with its rambling acres of exotic gardens, has remained a truly unique setting of southern history and horticulture. The opulent estate, beautifully nestled in the wooded hills of Northwest Georgia, was originally modeled from the published manuals of Andrew Jackson Downing, the premier landscape architect of nineteenth century America.

It all began with the magnificent creation of a wealthy British sea-merchant, Godfrey Barnsley, as a dream home for his beautiful Savannah wife, Julia Scarborough Barnsley.

During the early 1840's, they traveled three hundred miles north of Savannah, into the Georgia up-country and carved from an Indian wilderness, a vast estate and gardens they named "Woodlands." By the mid-nineteenth century, Barnsley had lavished a princely fortune on the wilderness Eden for his Julia. Hundreds of rare trees and shrubs, including redwoods, lindens, cunninghemias and ancient cedars of Lebanon, were imported from foreign lands to be planted at Woodlands. Also prominent among the gardens was one of the largest rare rose collections of the South, originally grafted from Celtic stock.

In the great Barnsley Manor, hand crafted windows were secured with sterling silver latches, and the towered entranceway provided breathtaking views of the rolling Georgia hills. Priceless furnishings collected from the four corners of the world filled the great structure, and the huge custom-built kitchen range easily cooked cuisine for one hundred and fifty guests. Wine and spirits, vented from Barnsley's arbors, bore the registered label of "Woodlands." The illustrious dream soon engulfed thousands of acres, to become one of the most flamboyant antebellum estates east of the Mississippi.

Its founder, sometimes referred to by ministers of trade as "Sir Godfrey Barnsley," (a gentleman of prominence title only) eventually became the wealthiest southern cotton factor and sea merchant of his time. From his seaport offices, and from the tower of Barnsley Manor at Woodlands, he directed a shipping empire that sailed the world seas and transported sixty percent of the South's cotton to his native England and other markets. Barnsley was also known for his strong principles of honesty and integrity in conducting international business, and his enterprises were highly respected by Ministers of Trade the world over.

Although Godfrey Barnsley preferred to remain a British subject, his contributions to America would prove to be quite significant. He became widely recognized for his distinctive methods of establishing U.S. Foreign Trade and served American Presidents as Vice-Consulate to European and South American nations. He would also be remembered for his valuable contribution to the development of Georgia's last wilderness frontier.

Godfrey's beloved Julia never lived to see the completion

of the illustrious dream, although four generations of her descendants would reside at Woodlands, until well into the twentieth century. By that time, the grand showcase estate had become commonly known as "Barnsley Gardens".

As the generations passed, Barnsley Gardens at Woodlands continued to stand like a bold monument against the ravages of time and the elements. Erected shortly after the final removal of the Cherokee Indian nation, it stood through the Great War Between the States, a tornado of 1906, the 1930's Depression, and now at the beginning of the 21st Century, is certainly a place where the past echoes loud and clear.

The Barnsley estate, however, was not only unique for its outstanding architecture and landscape. Through many years of research and interviews, I discovered hundreds of fascinating stories entwined with the Barnsley history that presented a most intriguing episode of old southern folklore. The Barnsley saga combines a century and a half of poignant love, adventure, misfortune and even murder. The fabulous manor and gardens had also been the setting for a best seller fiction novel of the 1800's, entitled ST. ELMO, written by the famous novelist, Augusta Evans Wilson, a friend of the Barnsleys. Many years later, according to early historians, and family associates, the young Atlanta writer, Margaret Mitchell, also became enchanted with Godfrey Barnsley's Woodlands. It seems she was especially intrigued by the colorful stories surrounding the daughter, "Julia", who struggled to preserve the estate through the Civil War and the period of southern reconstruction. Later, Mitchell's classic novel, "GONE WITH THE WIND" would echo themes of Julia's life at Woodlands.

There were also numerous legends of a mystical nature that had long lived at Barnsley Gardens. Down through the years, more than one wayfarer has claimed to have encountered the Lord of Barnsley Manor roaming the grounds. Some of the locals still insist that on special evenings at about the hour of dusk, the beautiful Julia Barnsley visits her marble fountain in the boxwood parterre.

Others claim that former residents of the manor have maintained an undying interest in the well being of the estate they loved and cherished for four generations. But regardless of their personal beliefs, or whether their stories have merit, one thing remains certain; the aged ruins of Barnsley Manor within its beautiful, romantic and mysterious setting tends to catch everyone in its spell. A visit to the historic "Downingesque" gardens creates a feeling of yesteryear that no one can forget. The scent of rare English box and heirloom roses linger in the memory long after leaving Godfrey Barnsley's Woodlands.

This story, derived from almost a lifetime of painstaking research and collecting of Barnsley memorabilia, is primarily based on family letters, diaries and business ledgers. It is also supported by literally hundreds of personal interviews, conducted with family members, former servants, and elder residents of the area from the early 1950's through the 1970's. Those people who were originally associated with the estate, and who have long since gone on to their rest, provided a great wealth of first hand information that could not have been obtained from any other source. To them, I owe many acknowledgments. Of course, I will always owe much gratitude to the merchant prince himself, for creating the beautiful Woodlands and for developing his own "letter press" upon which he copied and preserved many of his papers and memoirs. To his descendents, and family associates, who donated many of those to my collection over the years, I am also grateful.

In addition to this, some information was derived from state and national archives, university libraries, early historians, and many years of correspondence with Barnsley descendents in the U.S. and two foreign countries.

Due to the complexity of the unique Barnsley history, however, it would require much more than the pages of this

4

publication to provide a full and detailed story of the Barnsleys at Woodlands. Additional publications in the form of a novel and a screen play are planned for future release.

In this work, I have only attempted to present a simple narrative of major events surrounding four generations of this prominent "cotton" family of the South.

It should also be noted, that since Barnsley Gardens had become a sort of mystical phenomenon, I would find some of the legends associated with the estate to be either exaggerated or fictional. On the other hand, I would eventually uncover many factual stories, even stranger than fiction, that had never been revealed.

Therefore, I shall now take you on a brief journey through the colorful Barnsley history to unveil the true life to legend story of Barnsley Gardens at Woodlands.

The Author
Clent Coker

# CHAPTER 1

ORIGIN

On August 26, 1805, in the Peak Forest region of Derbyshire England, a male child was born to George and Hannah Barnsley. The Barnsley's healthy newborn was given the name Godfrey, in honor of his Father's brother, a prominent cotton broker of Liverpool, England. Young Godfrey was the third child of George and Hannah, having been preceded into the world by two older siblings, Joshua, and George Barnsley.

Although the Barnsley's were not of the royal blood lineage, they were considered to be among British families of prominence in the world of business and trade. George later stated in his own account, that he was a direct descendent of Reginald Barnsley, whose grandson John, had established the city of Barnsley England in Yorkshire.

It was there, in the late seventeenth century John had erected the family manor known as "Barnsley Hall" that has remained until the present day. Some of the family had moved from Yorkshire to Derbyshire in the early 1700's, and became involved in the business of cotton/mercantile. One branch of the family became craftsman of fine furniture, known throughout England as Gimson and Barnsley Company.

The Barnsley armorial bearings had been granted in 1597, with the motto "ut rosa sic vita" (life is like the rose).

Barnsley Coat of Arms

By the mid-1700's, cotton and yarn mills operating in Liverpool, Manchester, Belfast and Glasgow, had become an important part of Great Britain's economy. Young Godfrey's father, George, had previously gained some financial success as the owner/operator of a water-powered cotton mill. But in the late 1700's, when steam superceded the water powered mills, George Barnsley refused to change and his banks failed him. He soon returned to farming.

As young Godfrey grew up on the family farm, he was given the best education that his parents could provide, and proved to be a most intelligent child. Although he felt a certain appreciation for farming, and especially Botany, the one profession that seemed to intrigue him most was the business of cotton mercantile. At the age of fifteen, he had been sent to reside with his Uncle Godfrey in Liverpool, to be apprenticed at law. But the young Barnsley proved to show little interest in such a profession, and was soon allowed to be apprenticed as a clerk in his Uncle Godfrey's cotton "counting" house. He showed a great interest in the responsibilities of the business, and learned the trade so well, that within three years, he had become a chief clerk in his uncle's cotton brokerage.

By the age of eighteen, Godfrey had made up his mind to leave the land of his birth. He had reasoned that the real profits to be gained from the cotton business, was in the United States where most of the cotton was grown, for the British mills.

He also knew that according to British custom, his older brother, Joshua, would surely inherit what was left of the family estate, thus leaving him to earn his own fortune. Therefore, after receiving his Uncle Godfrey's blessings, along with a good letter of recommendation, he joined a cargo ship crew and worked his way across the sea to America.

Godfrey Barnsley first landed on American soil in the spring of 1824, at the bustling seaport city of Savannah, Georgia. According to early letters of correspondence with his relatives back in England, he was immediately charmed by the luxurious life style of the wealthy residents of Savannah. Along the winding waterfront, he could see the cheerful taverns overflowing with the rum and laughter of sea merchants, and the fancy coffeehouses accommodating the elite cotton factors of the city. Within the city boundaries, he discovered beautiful parks accented by huge mansions, theatres and magnificent ballrooms. But most interesting to young Barnsley were the numerous houses of business nestled on the high slopes above the Savannah River and the large mass of ships waiting in the harbor for a portion of Savannah's number one commodity, KING COTTON. To Godfrey, Savannah was truly an exciting city filled with great promise.

Godfrey's Childhood Home in England

9

Young Godfrey Barnsley

(Painted About 1822)

CHAPTER 2

A NEW LIFE

Shortly after his arrival in Savannah, Godfrey met a young man by the name of William Duncan and the two would become friends for life. William, being the son of a noted cotton factor, was naturally familiar with all the prominent merchants and their families in Savannah.

It was most likely the Duncan family who first introduced young Barnsley to Samuel Wright & Co., one of the largest merchants of the city. For it was only a short time later that Godfrey presented to Wright his letter of recommendation, and was hired to work among his staff of clerks.

In the months to come, Godfrey's work performance proved to be most satisfactory to Samuel Wright, who had discovered that Barnsley was extremely intelligent and dedicated to his business. He was therefore delighted to offer the young Barnsley a partnership in the company on June 15, 1826, of which Barnsley happily accepted. In the *"Savannah Georgian"* newspaper, dated June 20, 1826, Samuel Wright was quoted,

> *"This partnership is the natural outgrowth of the integrity and industriousness with which Godfrey Barnsley has approached his work and the "confidential" situation he has held with me since his arrival in Savannah."*

The new partnership proved to be very successful as Godfrey traveled frequently to the cotton planter's exchange in Augusta to secure new growers for the company. He would then return to his native England to establish new contracts for supplying the British mills with Georgia grown cotton.

Within his first two years in Savannah, Godfrey not only grew rapidly in the world of business, but in the city's civic and social circles as well. The handsome young Englishman with his dark complexion, brown eyes, and full locks of dark curly hair seemed to seldom go unnoticed by the young ladies of the city. He often attended the gala affairs sponsored by the merchants of "cotton factors row" and was remembered as cutting quite an impressive figure as he and the ladies strolled through the fancy ballrooms of old Savannah.

The young Britisher had soon decided that his new adopted city of Savannah would definitely be the place in which he would build his fortune.

By the year 1827, the city leaders had recognized Godfrey Barnsley as the most promising young merchant in the port of Savannah. One such leading and wealthy figure was Savannah's merchant prince himself, William Scarborough, II. It later became evident that Scarborough had kept his eye on the hard working young Barnsley, and was greatly impressed by his genuine perseverance in handling business for Samuel Wright and Co. Scarborough was a wealthy planter whose father had owned one hundred thousand acres of land and more than four hundred slaves across the Savannah River in South Carolina. In 1805, he had married Julia Bernard of Wilmington, North Carolina, and moved to Savannah where he acquired a fleet of ships and built a stately mansion that would become known as Scarborough Castle.

(Author's note: The castle still stands on King Boulevard overlooking the Savannah River. In 1997, it became the SHIPS OF THE SEA MARITIME museum.)

Scarborough Castle
(taken in 1935)
(Courtesy of Ships of the Sea Maritime Museum)

It was also William Scarborough, II, who had organized the Steamboat Company of Georgia on December 19, 1817, with a capital stock of $200,000, and produced the first steam-powered vessel (The Savannah) to cross the Atlantic Ocean. President James Monroe was one of the distinguished guests of Scarborough Castle and was on hand for the launching of the ships maiden voyage in May of 1819.

During the 1820's, the affluent Scarboroughs were hosts to many of the elite citizens of Savannah for parties and fancy balls held in the huge ballroom of Scarborough Castle. It was for one such gala affair that Godfrey Barnsley received an invitation, to which he readily accepted. He later remembered that he was received with real warmth and hospitality by Scarborough and his three daughters, Charlotte, Julia and Lucy. It seems they had already heard much of the social gossip concerning the young Britisher and were no doubt anxious to make his acquaintance. After an evening of dance and song, and the wine overflowing, Godfrey became quite enchanted by the Scarboroughs, and especially the second daughter, Julia (named for her mother) who seemed to have caught his eye from the very beginning. Attracted to both Julia's charm and her father's fame, young Barnsley began to visit the Scarborough mansion more frequently in the months that followed. By the spring of 1828, young Godfrey Barnsley had become romantically involved with Julia Scarborough.

However, Julia's mother, the affluent-leading lady of Savannah society, met the courtship with much opposition. Mrs. Scarborough was not at all pleased with her daughter being allowed to court a foreigner, and especially a Britisher, with no family or inheritance in Savannah. After getting to know young Barnsley, she highly disagreed with many of his ideals. She was especially concerned over him being a conscientious objector, thus refusing to serve in the Savannah militia along with the other young men of the city. Although he was a British alien, Barnsley had twice been forced to pay fines for failing to appear for military duty. Mrs. Scarborough was also quite disturbed to find that Godfrey had a completely foreign attitude toward slavery, and slave auctions, preferring to treat all commoners alike, whether Black, White, Indian or Irish. After all, slavery had been the very lifeblood of Savannah's labor force and if he intended to remain in the city, she felt he should conform to all of its customs. Mrs. Scarborough had reasoned that her daughter could have chosen to enter a courtship with any number of respectable young men descending from families of wealth and prominence in Savannah, rather than a strange and eccentric Britisher.

On the other hand, William Scarborough had seemed to pay little mind to the frustrations of his socially minded wife. He in turn, reasoned that most of the other young men of the city were only prominent because of their inheritance, instead of earning it on their own accord as young Barnsley was proving to accomplish. In spite of the pleas of Mrs. Scarborough, the courtship was allowed to continue.

William Scarborough II   *Julia Bernard Scarborough*

By the end of 1827, Barnsley had felt he was ready to begin building a solid foundation of business on his own account and decided to dissolve his partnership with Samuel Wright & Co. He sold back to Wright his half ownership in the sea vessel "Mary Lord" for the amount of $4,740, and then traveled from Augusta to New York and on to Liverpool to begin securing new accounts on his own behalf. It would be a business of operating on commissions only, so that Barnsley could ship cotton on behalf of the large Southern planters without having to invest his own funds to purchase and warehouse the product. He would, at first, lease ships from others, to transport and sell cotton to the foreign mills but would later purchase his own vessels.

Such foreign travels required much of Godfrey's time, although it seemed he was never too busy to spend some time with Julia, whenever he was in port. He returned to Savannah in the summer of 1828, with several pieces of jewelry he had purchased for her in New York, including one single pearl for which he paid $120.

The young sea merchant remained in Savannah throughout the summer while escorting the beautiful Julia Scarborough to numerous balls and social functions of the city. A close friend, Ashton Cox, had advised him to consider the matter very carefully before getting intimately involved with the affluent Scarboroughs. He claimed they were only concerned with "dress," and gadding about in a showy display of life, that would never bring Barnsley real wealth or true happiness. By this time, however, it had become evident that Godfrey was so in love with Julia, he totally ignored his friend's advice. The young Britisher soon became the highlight of the city's gossip circles when he announced his engagement to the beautiful daughter of the merchant prince of Savannah.

On December 24, 1828, Godfrey Barnsley and Julia Henrietta Scarborough were united in holy matrimony with best wishes from William Scarborough, family friends and many of the city's elite. Godfrey proved to be quite impressive, dressed out in his plum colored coat, embroidered by several of the society ladies of Savannah, and who also made Julia's lace ball gown and white satin Basque. But since mother Scarborough had not approved of the wedding, Godfrey handled most of the wedding expense himself, having Julia's trousseau made in Paris and London. The extraordinary wedding fete that took place in the Old Christ Church would remain one of the largest ever held in the port city of Savannah. The original wedding garments would remain in possession of the family for more than one hundred years.

Godfrey Barnsley

Julia Scarborough Barnsley

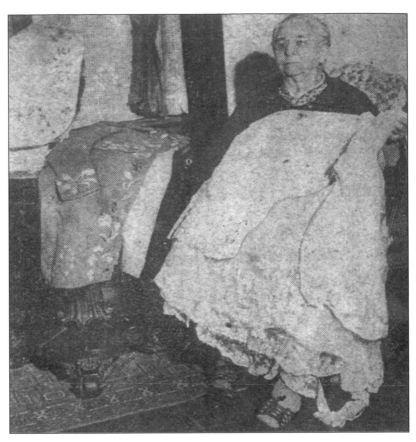

Barnsley's Granddaughter with
Original Wedding Garments

The young couple at first settled into an apartment in the
interim of the city, and Godfrey returned to his business, where
he vigorously indulged himself in building his new G. Barnsley
and Co. Enterprises. It was Barnsley's intention to operate
strictly under fair business practices, to build a good reputation
with both the planters and the buyers for foreign markets. He
was careful to personally inspect every load of cotton to be sure
of its good quality before accepting it for shipment and the young
entrepreneur soon became widely known for his honesty and

integrity. In 1829, Joshua Milne, a noted minister of trade in Manchester, England wrote to the owner of a new cotton business in Liverpool:

> *"You will no doubt find it necessary to have agents in all the principle southern ports of the United States. Under the circumstances, I have great pleasure in making you acquainted with Mr. Godfrey Barnsley, who operates a very extensive business in Savannah, and it gives me great pleasure to add that a gentleman possessed of more talent, assiduity and integrity I never knew."*

Barnsley's unique methods of handling business along with his outstanding knowledge of cotton became highly recognized by both the planters and buyers, and his business began to prosper. In his ledger from the ship, Tallahassee, dated January 17, 1829, Barnsley had recorded that it sailed for Liverpool, England with 1,711 bales of Sea Island cotton at a value of $60,000. By the spring of the same year, his company had cleared port for six more ships totaling more than $350,000, in Georgia grown cotton. Some of the ships used in his service at that time were: The Tallahassee, Emperor Champion, Salem, Tybee, Oglethorpe and his own two copper clad ships, the Olive and Eliza.

These ships not only produced him great profits from the transporting and selling of cotton, but also, for the fact the same vessels were returned to the United States, filled with European commodities. Barnsley was known to ship large cargos of wine, salt, carpeting and furniture, that also enabled him to earn large sums of money.

On some occasions, he personally invested in such foreign products and resold them in the States, earning even larger profits.

In the year of 1829, the G. Barnsley & Company shipped the first cargo of cotton from the United States to Norway, thus establishing the first cotton trade between the two countries. He in turn received, as a token of respect, from the Norwegian King, several pieces of fine furniture built by the most noted craftsmen of the day.

Barnsley experienced another fete of success in the year 1829, when President Andrew Jackson appointed him Vice Consul of the Netherlands, and later on that year, for the Kingdom of the Two Sicilies. His companies were expected to secure as much business as possible from the two countries, through the Port of Savannah and keep potential travelers informed of rules and regulations pertaining to them in the United States. The first announcement of this appointment appeared in the "Savannah Georgian" on June 8, 1829, as follows:

"The President has recognized Godfrey Barnsley of this city, as Vice Consul Ad Interim of the Netherlands for the Port of Savannah."

A short time later, Godfrey also became the President of Savannah's Chamber of Commerce. Such positions were quite an honor for young Barnsley, who was only twenty-four years of age and still a British subject. He would, however, prove to perform his duties well, maintaining the positions for many years. By 1830, due to his strong business ties with mother England, Barnsley had decided he could better serve American commerce by remaining a British subject.

The Barnsleys spent the first year of their marriage in England, since Godfrey found it necessary to remain there while establishing new accounts with the British mills. Their first child, a daughter, was born in England on October 14, 1829. She was christened Anna Goodwin Barnsley, in honor of her paternal grandmother. After spending a short time with his wife and new daughter, Barnsley departed the country to care for pressing business matters by again traveling to New York and back to Liverpool. Such trips usually required 28-30 days travel time each way, thus requiring him to spend much of his time on the high seas.

Meanwhile, back in Savannah, Mother Scarborough, although still at odds with her British son-in-law, was very proud and excited over her first grandchild. She soon wrote to Godfrey in England demanding that he bring Julia and the child back to Savannah and move them into the Scarborough house. Godfrey was, at first, reluctant to consider such a move, but on returning to the States a few months later, he honored her request, by moving his family into one wing of the castle.

By the beginning of the 1830's, The G. Barnsley and Co. Enterprises was growing at an unbelievable pace. But such had not been the case with the companies of William Scarborough! By that time, in fact, most of the Scarborough fortune had disappeared. Although his first steamship, The Savannah, had successfully crossed the Atlantic, breaking all records back in 1819, Scarborough had proved to be some years ahead of his time. It was apparent the world was not yet ready for large steam powered vessels to be used on the high seas. In 1832, The Savannah Steamship Company with Scarborough as its director and chief stockholder was forced into bankruptcy. But Scarborough had saved his "castle" by shifting it into the hands of a brother-in-law, to be held in trust for the Scarborough children. He then requested Barnsley to take over the management of the house and care for its upkeep, of which Barnsley agreed to do. For the next ten years, he would maintain the great house, paying the taxes and repairs, while also keeping up all the servants within its premises. He also built a third story onto the huge structure as a residence for his own family, and financed the education of Julia's two younger brothers,

Joseph and William Scarborough, III. According to Barnsley's ledger of expenses on the Scarborough estate, over a period of nine years, he spent some $10,000, of his own funds for such services.

It was during those years, that Godfrey Barnsley was considered the master of Scarborough Castle and its property. By this time, it was evident the Scarboroughs had became quite dependent on Godfrey Barnsley, although his domineering mother-in-law still refused to accept his strange "Britisher" ways. According to stories handed down through the family, it seemed that one of her main disagreements with Godfrey had stemmed from his carefree way of handling the family servants. On one occasion, while in the presence of a social guest, Mother Scarborough became infuriated at Godfrey for presenting a gold coin to one of the servants for some special deed he had rendered.

> *"Why, he treats them as though they're hired hands. The gossip will be raging all over the city, that we're having to pay our Negroes these days!"*

It seemed, however, that Godfrey considered the incident to be mere "poppycock." Apparently, he had finally learned to pay little attention to the social whims of his prideful mother-in-law.

Although Barnsley had accepted the fact that slave labor was the law of the day in the South, and that his wife Julia would soon inherit several of her own, he had never fully believed in the institution. Slave auctions were something Barnsley had detested since his arrival in the United States and he had refused to become involved in the business of slave trade. He had maintained that the country would someday realize that keeping a man bound for free labor would not prove to be profitable or bring real prosperity. To Barnsley, a man's labor was his talent and he should be paid for it accordingly. He also believed a worker would prove to be much more efficient under such an arrangement.

Barnsley would later take a few slaves into his domain and also received some as payments against debts, but they would prove to live within a civilized arrangement. They would be required to marry and maintain a moral lifestyle while rearing their own families, and residing in their own separate quarters, the same as hired hands. It would prove to be the only way he would accept the institution of slavery.

During the 1830's, while living at Scarborough Castle, Julia Barnsley gave birth to six more children. Their first son, Reginald, was born on May 24, 1831, but lived only two and a half years, dying of a respiratory ailment on November 1, 1833. The rest of the children were born in the following order: Harold (October 16, 1832), Adelaide (January 22, 1834), Julia (January 27, 1836), George (November 7, 1837 and Lucien (November 12, 1840).

It was also during the 1830's, that Julia had detected a respiratory ailment that seemed to be constantly irritated by the extreme heat of the low lands. During the summer of 1836, Godfrey had in fact, sent Julia and the children, along with mother Scarborough, to visit with friends in the cooler climate of Connecticut. On two more occasions, Julia accompanied Godfrey to England to spend some time in the native land of his childhood. It was there in the rolling countryside of England, they had first planned to build their dream home.

By the beginning of 1837, Godfrey Barnsley had amassed such a fortune that he was honorably considered the wealthiest cotton factor of the South. His books for 1835, showed that he had shipped more American grown cotton to Liverpool, Belfast, and Glasgow, than any other factor. During the year of 1835, for all of his businesses combined, he had cleared twenty-two ships through the Port of Savannah that returned him gross receipts in excess of $200,000.

Now that Godfrey was blessed with such wealth, he had fully decided it was time to move Julia out of Savannah, and return to the land of his birth, where he would build for her, the home he had planned. For several years he had been collecting and sketching his own plans of various Gothic type structures and landscaped gardens he had discovered bc⁺h in America and throughout Europe.

Also, as early as 1827, he had begun to show a keen interest in collecting objects of fine art and rare antiquities, from throughout Europe and other parts of the world.

One collection he had purchased included several pieces of antique furniture, a piano forte, an engraved portrait of Napoleon, an Eighteenth Century gold clock from Tulleries in Paris, rare china and silverware for which he paid a total price of $6175.84. Through the years, many more items were added to the list and carefully stored away in his Savannah warehouse, to be used in the home he would build.

There is much indication that Barnsley regretted moving his family away from Savannah where he had built his fortune. On the other hand, he was deeply concerned over Julia's health and believed the move was necessary. He also felt she would benefit greatly by getting away from all family influence. But Savannah had been good to Godfrey. Only nine years earlier, he had opened his first office on Savannah's "Cotton Factors Row" and now he had become one of the wealthiest men of the South. Therefore, in order to show his gratitude, he soon arranged with his wife and father-in-law to stage a very expensive ball that would serve as his farewell to Savannah. The spectacular three-day event held at Scarborough House in mid-March of 1837, filled the castle and overflowed into the streets until reaching the Savannah river front. Attending the grand event were both young people and old, including Judge Wayne of the United States Supreme Court, and of course all the very elite of Savannah society. The newspapers of the day described Barnsley as the master of the mansion who "with right old English hospitality" welcomed his friends and bade "the wine cup fly." The "Fancy Ball" proved to be such a success that later, a popular poem describing its activities, was written by Henry B. Anthony, a Governor of Rhode Island.

(Author's note: Godfrey Barnsley's "Fancy Ball" of 1837, cost him $20,000, and remains on record as one of the largest and most ornate balls ever held in the Port of Savannah.)

It was during the Fancy Ball however, an incident occurred that would forever change Barnsley's plan of building a home in the land of his birth.

In 1836, a financial panic had swept through Great Britain, causing many banks to fail, thus having a great effect on the cotton market. The account was later recorded in the memoirs of Godfrey's son, Dr. George Barnsley:

"It was while the Fancy Ball was in full swing, everyone happy and excited, that one of my father's ships arrived in port with his latest mails from Liverpool. They were soon brought into the city, to Scarborough House and my father quietly withdrew, hurriedly reading through his mail, only to discover that several of his largest accounts had suffered foreclosure and could not pay. Suddenly, he found himself in a critical financial situation. But due to his sternness, and eminent ability, he did not wince, nor groan, nor shed a tear, but only knew he would have to go to work again. He soon returned to the ball and entered once again into the activities which continued until morning."

In the days to follow, many of the factors and planters of the South were forced into bankruptcy. But, because of Barnsley's shrewd business acumen, he was able to weather the financial storm, remaining in Savannah for two more years, until many of those who had ruined him, came to his relief. By 1839, he had not only paid up all of his losses, but was well on his way to amassing even a larger fortune. It was then due to the fast growing popularity of the "Delta" grown cotton, he proceeded with negotiations to open additional offices in the seaport cities of Mobile and New Orleans.

Now that two more years had passed, and with Julia's health still threatened by the extreme heat, Barnsley felt the need more than ever to move her into a cooler climate, and build the home they had planned. Also, a very strange situation had arisen over the Scarborough property. Barnsley's father-in-law, William Scarborough had died in 1838, resulting in the eldest child, Charlotte Scarborough Taylor, demanding full control of the castle and all family matters. Although Barnsley had maintained the house, paying all of its expenses for the previous seven years; an indignant Charlotte Taylor made it very clear that the Barnsley's were living at the castle only because of her kindness to them. The disturbance she was causing in the family only seemed to worsen Julia's declining health.

Charlotte Scarborough Taylor
(Courtesy of Raymond Davis)

Since Barnsley's business was expanding so rapidly in the United States, he had by this time abandoned the plan of building a home as far away as England. At the suggestion of a friend, he looked into the possibility of buying a large farm near Zanesville, Ohio, but soon decided it would also be too far away from his ever-growing cotton business.

It was the following year that Godfrey was introduced to the newly evacuated Cherokee Indian lands lying in the beautiful Georgia up-country. Several of his Savannah associates had already began to settle there, and suggested to Barnsley it would be just the place in which to build his home. Among such friends was Charles Wallace Howard, a teacher and pastor of the Presbyterian ministry, and one of the founding fathers of Oglethorpe University. Howard had already started a home in old Cass County near the frontier trading post of Kingston that he named "Spring Bank." It was there, near a giant spring the Cherokees had called "Connessena," that Howard established the first school for the children of the new white settlers.

C.W. Howard of "Spring Bank"

Another was William Henry Stiles, who was well known throughout the state for having been appointed State Attorney General in 1836. Stiles had also purchased a considerable amount of land in the up-country and started a home overlooking the great Etowah River, that he called "Etowah Cliffs."

(Author's note: One hundred and thirty years later, the novelist, Eugenia Price, would release her Savannah trilogy, based on the life and times of William Henry Stiles at Etowah Cliffs.)

Etowah Cliffs

Others were Barnsley's long time friends, William Duncan and Francis Bartow, his Savannah business attorney, whose family had also purchased land in the area, near a place called "Cave Springs."

Thus it was, in the fall of 1839, that Godfrey Barnsley traveled with his friends through the narrow roads infested with wild animals and some disgruntled Indians, to view the beautiful up-country of Georgia's last Indian frontier. It was in the wooded hills of old Cass County, abundant with timber, graceful pasture lands, lush valleys and flowing springs, that Godfrey Barnsley felt he had found his promised land.

THE LAND LOTTERY

In 1802, the state of Georgia had ceded its North Western Indian lands, known as "Old Cherokee" to the federal government with the stipulation that the Indians would be removed from the area as soon as possible. By 1822, ten million acres of Georgia land in the northwest part of the state was still in possession of the Cherokee and Creek Indians. Georgia's Governor, George M. Troup soon demanded that the United States expel the Indians, or else the state agreement with the federal government would be considered null and void, leaving the state to take its own action of resistance. Finally, in 1825, a chief of the Creek tribe signed a treaty with the U.S. Government but since there were not enough tribal leaders in agreement with the treaty, it was never ratified and the state of Georgia immediately began to make a survey of the area.

In 1831, Governor Wilson Lumpkin of Georgia, ordered all of the Northwestern portion of the state known as "Cherokee" to be surveyed into four sections and laid off into land districts nine miles square. Thirty-three districts in the area were divided into 40-acre lots known as "Gold Lots," since it was believed they contained gold. Then sixty districts were laid off into 160-acre lots described as "land lots." There were a total of some 54,000 lots.

The state of Georgia wanted the area populated by white settlers as quickly as possible, and so by an act of its General Assembly on December 22, 1831, the state decided upon a land lottery. The lottery took place in 1832-1833, with only white males over eighteen and widows being qualified to participate. When drawn, the lots were sold from three to eighteen dollars with the stipulation that they must be deeded within five years from the drawing or they would be returned to the state.

By another act of the General Assembly, on December 3, 1832, old Cherokee was divided into ten counties, one of which was named "Cass" in honor of General Lewis Cass who had been a Governor of Michigan, as well as an early surveyor of Cherokee Indian affairs. The county seat, laid out in July of 1833, became known as "Cassville." During that time several agreements had been signed by small groups of Indians but where not accepted by the full tribal council. Finally, on December 29, 1835, the Cherokees assembled at New Echota, Georgia (near Calhoun in Gordon County), and decided on a treaty. The final agreement signed by Reverend J.F. Schermerhorn, and U.S. Commissioner William Carroll, ceded to the United States all of the remaining Indian territory east of the Mississippi, for a price of $5,000,000 and a guaranteed home in the western state of Oklahoma. Although there was much opposition from many of the Indians, and some members of Congress, the treaty passed the Senate by one vote and was signed by President Andrew Jackson on May 23, 1836.

Therefore, the notorious removal of the Cherokees, that became known as the "trail of tears," was forced upon them in the summer of 1838, by General Winfield Scott and seven thousand federal soldiers.

# CHAPTER 3

THE MOVE TO THE MOUNTAINS

It was with great anticipation that Godfrey Barnsley returned to old Cass county in 1840, and with the assistance of his friends, C.W. Howard and W.H. Stiles, began making arrangements to purchase land nearby. At that time, very few of the original drawers of land lots from the 1832 lottery had actually settled in the wilderness. Therefore, it was in the year 1840 that Barnsley and his associates contacted some of the owners of such lots, and began negotiating to purchase them. The first one hundred and sixty acre land lot (Lot No. 96) was purchased on June 30, 1841, and came from the original drawer, W.G. McBride, for which Barnsley paid $150. He soon purchased another one, (Lot No. 94) from G.W. Fish for $40. The deeds were made to Julia Barnsley's brother, Joseph Scarborough, to be held in trust for the Barnsley children.

Since Godfrey Barnsley was not an American citizen, most of the land he bought in Cass County was deeded to either Joseph Scarborough, or to his long time Savannah friend, William Duncan, to be held in trust for his wife and children. During the first decade, Barnsley would purchase twenty-two land lots, consisting of 3,520 acres for which he paid a total price of $5,150. In the years to come, he and his associates would purchase more land lots in the wooded hills of northwest Georgia.

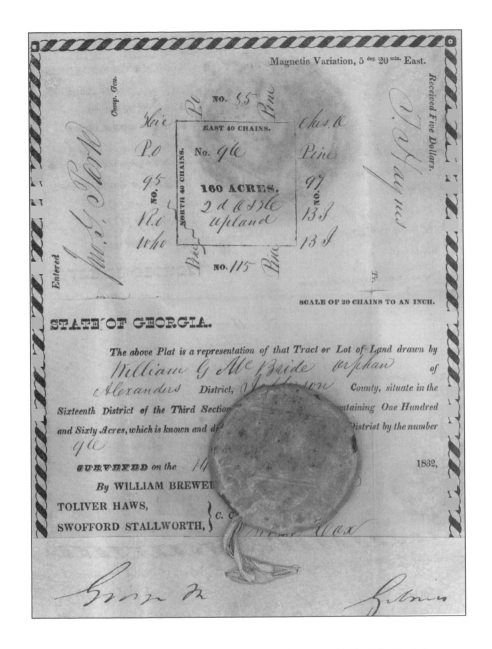

Magnetic Variation, 5 deg. 20 min. East.

NO. 55

EAST 40 CHAINS.

No. 96

160 ACRES.
2 d Osse
upland

NO. 115

SCALE OF 20 CHAINS TO AN INCH.

STATE OF GEORGIA.

The above Plat is a representation of that Tract or Lot of Land drawn by

William G McBride orphan of

Alexanders District, *Johnson* County, situate in the

Sixteenth District of the Third Section, containing One Hundred

and Sixty Acres, which is known and distinguished in said District by the number

96

SURVEYED on the *14* 1832,

By WILLIAM BREWER

TOLIVER HAWS,
SWOFFORD STALLWORTH, } C. C.

Original Land Lottery Deed from W.G. McBride

33

FINAL DEPARTURE

A short time later, Barnsley organized a wagon caravan, along with a large "coach and six," to transport his family and servants into the Georgia up-country. The entourage was led by an able bodied Irishman who was familiar with the Cherokee wilderness.

Their final departure from Savannah in the summer of 1841, seemed to cause quite a rage of excitement at Scarborough House. First of all, Julia's older sister, Charlotte, on discovering that most of the family servants preferred to follow her wealthy brother-in-law to the wilderness, had openly accused Godfrey of manipulating and disrupting the Scarborough household. But the Barnsley's would later prove her accusations were unfounded. They were very careful to select only the one-fifth of the family servants that Julia had rightfully inherited from her father, to be a part of their new household. Included were: Amos, Ben, Maria, Charlotte, Georgiana and a man named Moses, a trained bricklayer. Godfrey would later lease a slave carpenter by the name of "Woodson" from his close friend, William Duncan.

Also adding to the turmoil of their departure, was the fiery wrath of Mother Scarborough. She had become very distraught over watching her daughter and her grandchildren eagerly boarding the wagon train bound for the up-country. Once again, she lashed out at her son-in-law, accusing him of being an eccentric "Britisher" and completely barbaric for leading his wife and six children on the long and dangerous journey into the wilderness. She had felt there were still much better places within the civilized world he could have chosen to build Julia a home. Mrs. Scarborough had lamented that her daughter was a "high born Savannah lady," and not a mountain man's housekeeper.

On the other hand, Julia's sister Lucy, and her two younger brothers, along with many of the Barnsley's friends were on hand to bid them good-bye and wish them well with their new life on the new frontier.

The well equipped wagon train soon left Savannah on the treacherous three hundred mile trek into the Georgia up-country, traveling by way of Augusta, Covington, Terminus, (now Atlanta) until finally crossing the great Kennesaw Mountain into old Cass County. A full three weeks had passed when the long entourage finally reached the small trading post of Kingston, only five miles from Barnsley's new property.

At Kingston, the Barnsley's were happily greeted by their friend, Reverend C.W. Howard, who had made provisions for their lodging at his "Spring Bank" estate, until some quarters could be erected on Barnsley's land nearby. Mrs. Howard and her daughters, who had been living a rather secluded life in the country, were now very pleased that Julia Barnsley and her children would be living near them.

A few weeks later, Barnsley hired a local farmer and builder by the name of Edward Villers, who had decided he could do better to sell his small farm and go to work for the wealthy Englishman. It was Villers and several of the men servants that began cutting large trees from the forest to build the first crude log houses for the family and their servants until more efficient structures could be built.

Early Life in the Wilderness, taken in 1850's

THE INDIAN LEGACY

From family memoirs handed down from the older generations of Barnsleys and their servants, came the following story:

"It was one day while Villers and his workers were dragging logs through the woods, one of the Negro servants suddenly discovered a strange faced man peering from the doorway of a small, secluded cabin nearby. Barnsley was soon informed of the incident and immediately went into the woods to investigate the matter. Through an interpreter, he soon learned the old man was a Cherokee

Indian shaman who had lived there most of his life, and apparently he had been hiding out on the land since the Cherokee Indian removal, three years earlier. After a long visit with the Indian, Barnsley detected the man possessed a deep knowledge of the entire area. Realizing that such knowledge could be an asset to his estate, and also, not wishing to remove him from his original home, Barnsley invited him to remain on the property as long as he wished. He could stay on the land, work for Barnsley and be paid for his labor. The Indian eventually accepted Barnsley's offer.

(Author's note: Although the Cherokee nation as a whole had left Georgia by 1839, there were some members scattered over the territory who felt they could not survive the long journey west, and refused to leave. It seems there were a few who had preferred to hide out and take their chances of remaining on their native land, even if it meant eventually living under the white man's government. Actually, the majority of the civilized Cherokee nation had already taken up many of the white man's ways, with some owning huge plantations and large numbers of slaves. In fact, since the mid-1700's, they had been exposed to the Scotch and Irish settlers infiltrating their nation, and taking Indian women as their wives, until finally many of the Cherokees had a portion of the white man's blood coursing through their veins.)

However, the Indian shaman who had been hiding on Barnsley's property seemed to be guided by traditions from earlier times. For some months later, as the story was told, Barnsley decided to landscape a tall hill surrounded by two deep flowing springs, in which to build his proposed mansion and gardens, and the Indian became quite disgruntled over the matter. He immediately instructed Barnsley to choose another location on the property to build his home. He had believed the great hill and the deep spring in the valley below, was a sacred blessing from his forefathers and should not be disturbed. But Barnsley explained that he needed the water supply in order to survive, and could not change his plans. Neither did he feel anything special about the hill, other than its beauty or have any reason to believe in Indian superstition. Barnsley had thought the matter was finally settled and went on about his business. But a short time later the Indian disappeared and no one ever saw him again. Barnsley was somewhat puzzled over the incident but finally reasoned that the Indian must have gone west to join his people.

As the years passed, the account of the old shaman would become one of the mystical legends of Barnsley folklore, known as the Barnsley Indian curse.

(Author's note: Shortly after the turn of the 20th century, when a newspaper reporter was covering a misfortunate event that had occurred on Barnsley's land, he somehow learned of the story surrounding the Indian. He soon printed the story in his newspaper, adding that Barnsley had been cursed by the Indian because of disrupting a sacred Indian burial ground; a story that would follow the family for generations to come. I felt, however, the story needed some further explanation.)

In an interview with Molly Curtis (age 102) in 1959, concerning the proposed curse, she offered the following:

"Oh yes, I remember the folks at Barnsley talking bout that old Indian man…and I still remember

that little log house they said he used to stay in too...played around it when I was a child, course I never seen em... he was done gone by then. They said, he put up some kinda fuss with Mistuh Barnsley bout usein his Indian land...and I heard my mammy say, 'he didn't want no body usein outta that big spring down the hill'. But Mistuh Barnsley say he pay it no mind, went on and used it anyway... Well, they said some of the Barnsley children went down thah snoopin' round his place one day, and found out he was gone! Wasn't no trace of that Indian. His hoss, his dog and everything was gone... never did come back no more. Guess it was just as well, cause he was mighty strange they said. But now, I don't know nothing bout no curse you talk about, no suh, Mistuh Barnsley was mighty good to us... had lots o'good times growing up thah. Don't know nothin bout no curse."

(<u>Author's note:</u> During my childhood, several of the elderly residents of the area told the same tale concerning the Indian. But during all the years of research, I was never able to gather any further information concerning the Barnsley Indian legend.)

Many years later, two leaders of the Cherokee nation, Richard Bird and A.B. Running Horse would visit the Barnsley estate to investigate the long proposed Indian curse. Both of the native Americans stated that Cherokees did not practice placing curses on people. But as a token of respect for the beautiful estate, they would perform a ceremonial peace dance, showing that a peaceful serenity was reigning over Barnsley's land, which they stated was in perfect harmony with all of the Cherokees.

CHAPTER 4

PLANNING THE ESTATE

Godfrey Barnsley was able to spend a considerable amount of time with his family in the wilderness during the years 1841-42, since his chief clerks were temporarily caring for the cotton business on the seaports. It was while living in the first crude log house that Barnsley directed Ed Villers in landscaping the huge acorn shaped hill, high above the Indian springs. A large portion was leveled off into an area 60 x 80 yards for a proposed formal garden. The remainder of the hill was carefully landscaped into a series of terraces upon which the tallest would be the prominent setting for his proposed mansion and other family structures. It was while pouring through the many plans and drawings he had sketched during his world travels, and from a treatise on country architecture and landscape gardening (published in 1841, by Andrew Jackson Downing), that he laid out the construction plans for the home and gardens. The landscaping venture proved to be quite an undertaking that cost him $540.

THE DOWNING CONCEPT

Godfrey Barnsley had been greatly impressed by the publications of A.J. Downing, who was considered the "premier" landscape architect of nineteenth century America. Born in 1815, Downing was the son of a horticulturist who had established a botanical garden and nursery at Newburg, on the Hudson River, north of New York City. When Andrew was still in his teens, he became very interested in horticulture and joined with his family in expanding the business establishment. At the early age of seventeen, he began writing and publishing articles that would prove to have a powerful effect on architecture and landscape gardening in America. By the mid-1840's, his "treatise" on landscape gardening adapted to North America, had become so widely recognized, that it was considered to be only second in popularity to the Holy Bible itself. The "treatise" was followed by many other publications that also made a great impression on Americans such as, THE JOURNAL OF RURAL ART AND RURAL TASTES, THE ARCHITECTURE OF COUNTRY HOUSES, (with a reference to Gothic revival and picturesque landscapes), A PLAN FOR COTTAGES AND VILLAS and also a publication on fruit trees of America.

It was Downing who taught Americans how to civilize and beautify their surroundings by recommending architectural embellishment to effect a union between house and grounds. He was later commissioned by the government to design the grounds of the United States Capitol, and the new Smithsonian Institute. It was also Downing who personally spearheaded the new movement for public parks in American cities.

However, the concepts of A.J. Downing and his business partner, the noted British architect, Calvert Vaux, presented a Gothic and Italianate design that was hardly accepted by most

Southerners, since it was in complete contrast to the "Greek revival" style that had became the symbol of Southern aristocracy. But Godfrey Barnsley had been thoroughly intrigued with the unique Downingesque concepts he had discovered while traveling through New England, where most of the Downing style structures, and gardens were being erected. Such magnificent landscapes, no doubt, reminded him of the fine English countryside from the days of his boyhood.

In the years to come, Godfrey would follow almost every aspect of the Downing technique in building his North Georgia estate. He would however prove to be one of the very few to introduce such concepts to the old South.

THE FIRST STRUCTURES

The first family dwelling that Barnsley erected on the upper terrace of the newly landscaped hill was a large wood frame structure that would later become one wing of the mansion he would build. According to his estate ledger, the 38 x 42 ft. structure that was called "the new house," cost him $800.

From the very beginning, Barnsley had planned his estate to be a self-supporting farm. Therefore, as soon as land could be cleared for a new road opening onto his property, he arranged for his freight wagons to bring in from Terminus (Atlanta, 60 miles south) and the town of Rome, (fourteen miles west), a variety of new farm tools and implements, along with extra mules and several teams of oxen. The workers were soon able to erect a blacksmith shop and Barnsley later transported from Augusta, a steam powered sawmill that would prove to aid them tremendously in the construction.

Since Barnsley's servant, Moses, was experienced in the art of brick making, he soon erected his own kilns and began gathering clay from a local hillside, to manufacture bricks for the project. As soon as the kilns began to produce, a sturdy brick building was erected over one of the natural springs in the deep valley below. The "spring house" was the first, and most important service building to be erected on the property, since it provided fresh drinking water, and a cool storage area for food perishables, that was necessary for the family and servants to survive.

The following is a list from the first building expenses on the estate:

Cost Sheet from ledger:

Log house	$ 500
Spring house	250
Outhouses *And corn cribs*	500
Clearing 60 acres	480
New house	800
Terrace/Gardens	540
Total	$3,070

Barnsley soon arranged for a wagon train to bring up from Savannah, some pieces of furniture, and necessary household items to be installed in the new house.

It was while living in this house, that plans were drawn for another large dwelling to be erected on the upper terrace, about thirty yards directly across from the first house, that would serve as the kitchen and servants quarters. It was designed to be a 40 x 40 foot brick structure, featuring a billiard room and a dining room, along with a full basement to be used as a wine and brandy cellar. The kitchen was destined to be another wing of the great mansion that would dominate the main portion of the upper terrace in the years to come.

In the spring of 1842, Ed Villers took charge of planting the first crops, and Barnsley hired a young and energetic Irishman by the name of John Connolly to be the first manager over his new estate. Connolly would serve him faithfully for many years.

Although living in the wilderness proved to be quite an emotional change for Julia, Godfrey felt he could eventually make her life easier there and her health would greatly improve in the cool and peaceful mountain air.

The Barnsleys were indeed proud of their new land. They soon named the estate, "Woodlands," a title they felt was quite fitting, since it was lying isolated in the heart of an Indian wilderness.

CHAPTER 5

LIFE ON THE FRONTIER

Julia Henrietta Barnsley was only thirty-two years of age when she gave birth to her eighth child, Godfrey Barnsley, Jr., born in the wilderness on July 29, 1842. Julia was attended by a midwife from the W.H. Stiles plantation along with her personal servants, who also cared for the younger children, while she recuperated from childbirth.

A few weeks later, the Barnsley's school age daughters were sent to "Spring Bank" near Kingston, to attend Reverend C.W. Howard's newly established private school.

In an early brochure, Reverend Howard had advertised that his school would be limited to twenty girls, and all were to sleep in the Howard house, eating together as members of one family, with complete seclusion being the essential principle. Since they were expected to keep their thoughts strictly in their studies, the children were not allowed to visit their homes more often than once a month. But church and Sunday school attendance was expected of each one.

The tuition was $15 for a five-month session for the ordinary branches of education, and $20 per session for the higher branches, such as the languages, Science and the Classics. The cost for board and lodging, which included a comfortable bathhouse, was $9 a month in advance.

The Barnsleys were indeed pleased to have such a school near their "Woodlands" estate, and Godfrey would soon show his appreciation by rendering Rev. Howard a considerable amount of financial assistance. On November 5, 1842, Howard wrote to Barnsley, kindly requesting him to bring from England, some necessary supplies for the operation of the school, and some items of clothing for his Negroes. Barnsley saw to it that Howard received the items as soon as they could be transported into the wilderness. In another letter, Howard had asked Barnsley to finance the building of a church he wanted to establish nearby, of which Barnsley quickly obliged. He provided Howard $1200, from his own funds to establish the new church near "Connesena," about halfway between Spring Bank and Woodlands.

Some years later, he would also provide Howard the funds to establish a church on Barnsley land that would one day become known as the Barnsley Methodist Church. During those early years, Godfrey Barnsley also cared for the needs of many others living on the frontier. By means of his ships, he had access to the world markets, and began transporting for his Cass County neighbors, and to the local trading posts, many rare necessities that were not otherwise available in the up country. While such transactions were always noted in his ledgers, there is no record that he ever charged any type of commission for such deeds.

In the fall of 1843, Barnsley's friend, W.H. Stiles, who had just been elected to the House of Representatives, asked Barnsley to back a financial arrangement for extra land he wanted to purchase near his Etowah Cliffs plantation, twelve miles south of "Woodlands." Stiles offered Barnsley five slaves as security, of which he accepted.

Barnsley also showed genuine concern for those of his own household who had proved their loyalty while settling the wilds of the frontier. On one occasion, when writing from Liverpool,

England, he instructed his overseer, John Connolly:

"Burn more bricks in the kilns as soon as possible,
to build new houses for Amos and Uncle Moses."

Since they were still residing in the first crude cabins, Barnsley feared they might suffer during the up coming winter. He also felt they would fare better generally while living in sturdy houses of their own.

Godfrey Barnsley had truly proved to be a significant trailblazer in settling the Cherokee country, along with providing much assistance to his Cass County neighbors. But he would also experience some unpleasantness while building his home in the wilderness. It was evident that some of the smaller farmers on the frontier were envious of his great wealth and influence and considered him a threat to their welfare. Since he continued buying up much of the land in the area, one of the frontiersmen had referred to him as, "That damn John Bull Englishman." According to the account of an early neighbor, Mrs. Nancy Green, the man had stated:

"Why, he's buying up the whole territory, and the
next thing you know, he'll be controlling
everything."

On at least two occasions he was scorned for his peculiar method of handling servants, requiring his slaves to marry and rear their own children within a civilized family arrangement. Barnsley had, in fact, became well known for such principles.

In one letter to his family, concerning a servant, he wrote:

"I shall be pleased for you to select from the cellar,
two bottles of old Madeira for Elisha's wedding."

On another occasion, he wrote to his overseer, John Connolly, requesting that he furnish a fine Christmas dinner for all of his servants and their families.

A land overseer of a small plantation nearby had feared that once the other Negroes of the area learned of Barnsley's methods, it would cause a local slave rebellion, as he lamented:

> *"He's ruining the Negroes, treating them like white hired hands. With all the wealth and influence he has, we will see a slave uprising for sure!"*

The Barnsley's however, proved to have a much better relationship with their servants than did many of the other landowners of the area. A close friend, Charles Green, of Savannah who had visited Woodlands, wrote to Barnsley concerning his household:

> *"You are fortunate in your domestics, a more orderly and subordinate little colony I never saw...and that is no small solace in these turbulent times."*

Although Barnsley would continue to experience some prejudice and ridicule, he intended to show the raw frontiersman that he was an English gentleman, and was still determined to create a beautiful estate in the wilds of the North Georgia mountains.

During the 1840's, Barnsley's estate continued to grow and prosper with the rest of the county. Some of the original drawers of land lots from the 1832 lottery had begun to set up homesteads and farm their lands. Some of those who had descended from "Cherokee" blood had remained to reestablish themselves into the white man's way of life, with some becoming farmers for the larger white landowners.

In the year of 1843, Barnsley found it necessary to spend more of his time with business in Savannah, and also a trip to Liverpool to meet with his foreign accounts. It was on that return trip from England, that he brought with him the first load of his fabulous furnishings for Woodlands. Since the railroad had been extended north from Terminus (Atlanta), to Cass County in 1843, he was able to transport many items of interest, including a boxcar load of rare English box, and other exotic plants to begin setting out the various gardens he had planned. Also included among the items was a large custom built stove Barnsley had personally designed to cook for one hundred and fifty guests. The huge stove, built by the noted craftsman J. Holgate of Liverpool, would later dominate one room of the kitchen wing. Barnsley was met at the railroad by his own fleet of ox-drawn freight wagons that would transport the tremendous collection of fixtures across the last twenty miles of rugged roads through the wilderness. Barnsley was indeed lavishing a fortune on his grand estate, and Julia was beginning to enjoy her new life in the cool refreshing air of the Georgia up-country.

However, while following their beautiful dreams, the Barnsley's would also experience some misfortune. Woodlands was struck by its first tragedy when Godfrey Barnsley, Jr., their last and only child born on the frontier, suddenly became a victim of lung fever. Since he was too ill to be transported from the wilderness, and there were no doctors near Woodlands, the child died on July 30, 1843. Although Julia's health had been improving in the up-country, the death of her baby son would prove to be a setback to her physical and mental well being, for some time to come. A grieving Godfrey, and his overseer, immediately cleared ground on a small knoll 200 yards southeast of his prominent hill, to establish the first cemetery at Woodlands.

In order to ease the responsibility Julia felt for the rest of her young children, Godfrey rearranged the situation by hiring a live-in tutor for his sons, Harold and George. The eldest daughter, Anna, was sent to Montpieler College near Macon, Georgia, to begin classes for the year 1844, while daughters, Julia and Adelaide, remained at the Spring Bank school near Kingston.

Godfrey was now more eager than ever, to begin the dream castle for his Julia. By once again studying the many plans he had sketched over the years, he consequently drafted the final floor plan and started the foundation for a huge sixteen-room edifice that would eventually become the grand Barnsley Manor.

(Author's note: A study of the original plans revealed that Godfrey Barnsley was not only a prosperous cotton factor, and shipping merchant, but also a gentleman architect of considerable merit.)

The entire landscape surrounding the great house would feature a variety of gardens, including a large oval boxwood parterre, with serpentine walks, rockeries and fountains, thus presenting the distinctive style of A.J. Downing, and the international tastes of Godfrey Barnsley.

His plans also called for several other gardens, orchards, and vineyards that would be planted around the landscaped hill and throughout the valleys below. In January of 1842, he had ordered from the D. Landreth and Fulton Co. of Philadelphia the following trees: Apples, Apricots, Almonds, Cherry, English Walnut, Filbert, Gooseberry, Quince, Peaches and Spanish Chestnut. He had also ordered many varieties of the rose, rhododendrons and other flowering shrubs. These were set out along the upper terrace between the new house and the kitchen wing, surrounding the foundation that was being laid for the great manor.

Meanwhile, during the year of 1843, Julia had been receiving letters from her mother in Savannah, who seemed to want to make peace with her daughter and son-in-law. It was also evident that Mother Scarborough was very eager to visit with her grandchildren that she had not seen in over two years. Therefore in the late fall, Godfrey arranged for his mother-in-law to come to Woodlands to spend some time with the children while Julia would accompany him on a trip to Savannah, to visit with her sister, Lucy. In early 1844, Mrs. Scarborough dictated a letter to be sent to her family back in Savannah describing her first trip into the up-country and to update Julia on the work going on at Woodlands. It read in part:

"While first traveling the state road going up toward Tennessee, it took more than two weeks from Savannah to Cass County. As we finally passed over the Connesena, through the wilderness to Woodlands, some of the people in their cabins seemed alarmed at the sight of our large carriage. I find this up-country to be so different, roaming with wild animals and the wolves so numerous, and very troublesome for eating the young pigs and lambs. But the place is becoming more beautiful every day and very pleasant. Mr. John Connolly, the overseer and gardener improves the grounds around the log cabins and the first habitations of Woodlands. The "New House" is now well furnished with some elegant pieces, and the table is always bountiful in venison, wild turkey, birds and fish. This wilderness swarms with wild game, and there is no end to singing birds, geese, cranes, ducks, wild pigeons and others beautifully feathered."

Mrs. Scarborough's letter

Mother Scarborough returned to Savannah in the spring of the year to reside with her son, Joseph.

Later that year, the planting of the formal gardens had progressed so well that Julia wrote to her husband at his office in Savannah:

> *"John Connolly is very busy with the huge boxwood parterre, and the serpentine walks look very grand; they will be beautiful when the hill is finished."*

During the year of 1843, Barnsley had been well pleased with the building of Woodlands, although the cotton market had shown a considerable decline during the last quarter of the year. Barnsley's partner, John Day, who represented their firm in Liverpool, had wrote to him on February 3, 1844:

> *"At this time, the market is very unsettled. Due to an excess of cotton on hand, the price has dropped three-eighths of a pence per pound, lower than ever recorded on the English market."*

Godfrey now found it necessary to travel frequently between his offices in both the United States and Great Britain, to secure new commodities for shipping, thus leaving his family and estate in the care and keeping of his overseer, John Connolly. But during his long absences, Julia became very lonely. Although she was ably assisted by Connolly and the servants, her loneliness for her husband, along with the recent loss of her baby son had only seemed to contribute more to her distress and declining health. In June, she wrote to Godfrey, who had just returned to Savannah from a lengthy trip to New Orleans:

"The children want to see you as much as I do. Pray make haste in returning to Woodlands. I have been completely cheated this year, going on eight months since I have had the pleasure of seeing you."

One of Julia's Lonely Letters

Godfrey was likewise frustrated over having to leave Julia in the wilderness for such long periods of time. But feeling sure that he was getting his business in good order, he wrote:

"It will only be a short time until we fully enjoy completing Woodlands together. I shall never forget our many happy days together. Believe me, now more affectionately yours than when we met before the altar a long time ago."

During the summer months, Julia's health had seemed to improve. But the cold damp winter that followed seemed to take its toll. She had become frail and nervous and many of her days were spent in pain. Godfrey had wanted her to come to Savannah where her original physician, Dr. Arnold, could treat her. But due to all the gossip and turmoil that was still raging over the Scarborough property, she had seemed to build up an uneasy feeling toward the entire area and preferred not to be seen there.

Although Barnsley regretted being away from his family through much of 1843-44, his travels did prove to aid him financially. While suffering from a drop in cotton, he had managed to secure other commodities for shipping, so that his books for 1844, showed a personal income of $51,114.73. But much of the money earned that year was spent toward the support of the Scarborough household back in Savannah, and to pay the taxes on Scarborough Castle although Charlotte Taylor had taken over the house. Godfrey's brother-in-law, Joseph Scarborough had already written to him on October 6, 1843:

"I found the castle so hot and the atmosphere so unpleasant that I left there, and if something isn't done, the house is going to ruin fast."

In September, 1844, he wrote again to say that Mother Scarborough had "had enough" of Savannah and asked if she could come to live at Woodlands. He had hoped that Godfrey could find her a small farm in the mountains.

By this time, it seemed that Mother Scarborough had finally decided to "bury the hatchet" she had long carried for her British son-in-law. Apparently, she had finally become reconciled to the fact that Godfrey had, proved to be a true friend and the financial savior of her household. Also, after suffering from all the turbulence over the Scarborough dispute that had forced her removal from the house, it was apparent she needed Godfrey and Julia more than ever. Since Godfrey felt her presence would possibly lift Julia's spirits a bit, he arranged to have Mrs. Scarborough and two of her servants moved to Woodlands in the fall of 1844.

Mrs. Scarborough's presence did seem to help fill Julia's loneliness, and she decided to remain at Woodlands, to care for her ailing daughter and her grandchildren.

Nevertheless, as the harsh winter of 1844 progressed, Julia suffered another attack of nervousness and lung ailment, coughing almost constantly. Since there was no physician near Woodlands, and Mother Scarborough was there to care for the younger children, Julia finally decided to join Godfrey in Savannah. Shortly after welcoming in the New Year of 1845, she was taken to the railroad at Cassville, and while accompanied by her friends, Mrs. Howard and Mrs. W.H. Stiles, boarded the train to Savannah. Soon after her arrival to the home of a friend there, Barnsley wrote to his mother-in-law, back at Woodlands:

"She is looking much worse than I expected, and I am surprised she has been able to come down at all. On Monday, she suffered dreadfully on the railroad and was unable to walk, but can now

move about a little. But Drs. Hollock and Arnold have attended her and after their examination, gave a favorable account of her lungs, stating her diseases arise chiefly from dyspepsia. She is being kept as comfortable as she can be. Repose and attention will, I trust, bring her around again."

Toward the end of January, 1845, Julia's condition had shown some improvement, so that Godfrey was able to leave her for a brief trip to Woodlands. His primary reason for the trip was to encourage John Connolly and his workmen to hasten with the building of the large brick mansion for Julia. Within a few days however, he began receiving letters from Savannah, telling of the sudden seriousness of his wife's condition. A friend, Mrs. Reid, wrote:

"Mrs. Barnsley would have written herself this evening, but is rather unwell from one of her nervous attacks, which she has been troubled with lately."

Since Barnsley was well accustomed to Julia's spasms of nervousness, it seems that he was not overly concerned of the news, until receiving another letter two days later. On February 10, his partner, John Day wrote:

"Sorry to say, Mrs. Barnsley's health is much worse. Since your departure, she has become much weaker. Dr. Arnold says she is in a very doubtful state and recommends for you to come down at once."

Barnsley received Mr. Day's letter on February 15 and left at once for Savannah, but only to arrive a few hours late.

Julia Barnsley died on February 16, 1845, at only thirty-five years of age. Godfrey Barnsley's entire world had suddenly crumbled beneath him. Never would he be able to forgive himself for not being at Julia's side during her last hours. Deeply shocked, a grieving Barnsley interred his wife, in the vault of a Scarborough relative, Robert Issac, at the old colonial cemetery in Savannah. It was the same vault in which her baby son, Reginald, had been buried thirteen years earlier. Friends and relatives in both Savannah, and Cass County, were deeply saddened.

Barnsley's eldest daughter, Anna, 16, was so grief stricken that she gave up her schooling at Montpelier College and returned home to help care for her younger siblings.

Within a few weeks, Barnsley placed his business fully in the care of his partner, John Day, and left for the up-country to be with his children, for now the family needed each other more than ever.

CHAPTER 6

THE YEARS OF HEALING

After the death of Julia, Godfrey Barnsley began to show rather drastic changes in mood and temperament. Even his children began to notice the change in his personality and that he seemed to view life much more seriously. It was while spending time at the homestead with his children, that his loneliness for Julia became even stronger, and he decided, rather suddenly, to abandon the idea of completing the grand manor. After all, Julia was gone, and as far as he was concerned, nothing would ever again be the same at Woodlands. John Connolly and the servants were given orders to farm the lands for family sustenance until more important decisions could be made. As soon as family matters were fairly under control, Barnsley left Woodlands for Liverpool, by way of New York, and would not return for some time.

While still filled with grief and somewhat driven by mixed emotions, Barnsley spent the following months traveling constantly between his seaport offices at New Orleans, Savannah and Liverpool, until finally settling down at his office in Mobile. It was there he joined with two new partners, James and Edmund Sager to form a cotton commission business under the name of Barnsley, Sager & Co. of Mobile. Gradually, he began to transfer his business operations away from Savannah, to the ports of Mobile and New Orleans. He also resigned his position as President of Savannah's Chamber of Commerce, much to the regret of the city's business and civic leaders.

When a year had passed after Julia's death, the lonely Barnsley was encouraged by his business partners in Mobile, to attend one of the large social functions of the city. Godfrey had attended very few public gatherings after his wife's death, since such gala affairs only seemed to remind him of his happier days with her. Also, after Julia's death, Barnsley often became annoyed by the widows and single ladies at such gatherings who seemed eager to make his acquaintance due to his prominent standing and especially his great wealth. But after being reminded by the Sager Brothers that his presence before the city's elite would strenghthen their new business venture, the "Merchant Prince" agreed to attend a fancy ball, held at Mobile's famous Alhambra Hotel on February 24, 1846.

The ultimate reason for his invitation to the ball, however, turned out to be something much different than Barnsley had anticipated. For it was then that the wife of his partner, Edmund Sager, introduced Barnsley to a clairvoyant, or spiritual informant, who suggested that his loneliness for Julia, could be eased by having proper spiritual communication with her. He was soon persuaded by Mrs. Sager, who also professed to be a "spirit medium," to allow a brief encounter with the informant. Although Barnsley was somewhat impressed with the experience, and accepted from Sager a printed publication pertaining to "life after death," he was still not convinced of such a theory.

(Author's note: The American spiritualistic movement that was later established in Hydesville, New York, in 1848, had already seemed to be gaining momentum in the ports of Mobile and New Orleans. It would soon become a popular movement with various "mediums" writing and receiving spirit letters that circulated the nation until the late 1860's.)

Meanwhile, Barnsley returned to the daily tasks of life and business in Mobile, that now posed two main problems. First of all was his concern for the care of his family living in the North Georgia Mountains, hundreds of miles from Mobile. Although Barnsley had shown little interest in returning to Woodlands after Julia's death, he was often frustrated over having to be so far away from his rapid growing children, and especially his eldest son, Harold, who he felt needed a father's guidance more than ever. It seemed that all the children had longed for their father during his long absences. George, who was ten years old, had wrote to his sister, Julia, at Spring Bank school stating that he sure wished his Papa would write since he had not seen him in a long time. Anna, at the age of seventeen, who was still assisting her Grandmother Scarborough in caring for the younger children, had wrote to her father in Mobile:

> *"I had hoped that we could all spend the summer together at Woodlands;...You are now the only one I have to gratify; therefore my prayer to God morning and evening is that I may be able to do so."*

A short time later, Barnsley became quite disturbed over a letter from John Connolly stating that Anna had been receiving gentlemen visitors, although they had seemed respectable. She had also wanted the carriage cleaned and painted to attend a party at one of the colleges in Cassville. In the meantime, Mother Scarborough had wrote to Barnsley, describing the rest of his children as follows:

> *"Julia is the smartest and made for the ups and downs of life...She is such a saucy little independent and is forever in some scrape or other,*

61

*just like her grandmother. Adelaide will be tall, I
think and is progressing rapidly to womanhood
and will make a handsome woman and a good
housekeeper.*

*George is trying very hard to learn but so slow
with it...He will be a noble looking man. Lucien
will be a great orator, and is very active and loud.
Harry is like Uncle Joe, and when he sows his wild
oats will make a good man."*

The second main problem facing Barnsley since he had
now moved his main shipping firm away from Savannah, was
his concern for the hundreds of valuable furnishings and
collections of art that he had been storing there for a number
of years.

On April 13, 1846, John Day wrote from Savannah, stating
that there were still one hundred and thirty-one crates, in
addition to many pieces of imported marble statuary and a large
collection of art, stored in a warehouse there. Since the Western
& Atlantic Railroad had been completed to Kingston, in 1845,
he could have shipped them to the up country, but there were
still not enough buildings at Woodlands, to store them properly.
Barnsley knew that he would soon have to decide between two
factors, either to direct John Connolly in constructing more
buildings at Woodlands, and have tutors brought in for his sons,
or else, move his entire family to the Port of Mobile, where he
could watch over them better. With such matters weighing
heavy on his mind, Barnsley left Mobile rather suddenly,
traveling by stage to Montgomery, where he boarded a train to
Atlanta, and on to Kingston station for a brief visit to his
Woodlands estate.

On arriving at Woodlands, he was pleased to find both his
family and the estate had fared rather well under the efficient

care of John Connolly and the servants. In his daily journal, he noted that the flower gardens were beginning to blossom beautifully and the farms had prospered well, so that the cribs were filled with corn, potatoes, ground nuts and peas, providing the family with plenty of food. The family servant, Amos, had tended a full two acres of vegetable gardens, and the orchards and vineyards were beginning to produce excellent fruitage. He also noted that his livestock herds were expanding rapidly.

Although Barnsley had found it extremely difficult to face his unfinished dream without Julia, his tensions were somewhat eased over finding such favorable conditions on the estate. He, therefore, decided to remain for a while in the cool peacefulness of Woodlands, and take some time to reflect before making his final decisions.

A NEW ENCOUNTER

It was while relaxing one afternoon in the formal gardens at Woodlands, that Barnsley received a rather strange and interesting visitor. A Mrs. C.V. Berrien, originally of Mobile, who had since moved to Rome, Georgia, abruptly confronted Barnsley, stating that she had been directed to him through a spiritual informant. Although Mrs. Berrien had not previously been acquainted with Barnsley himself, she seemed well aware of his loneliness for Julia. After finally convincing Barnsley to accept a brief spiritual encounter, she suggested that he was endowed with certain spiritual powers, that would allow him to communicate with his deceased Julia. The mysterious Mrs. Berrien then left Woodlands, rather suddenly, just as she had came. A startled Barnsley soon began pouring through the pages of Mrs. Sager's Book on "Spirit Communication" he had received back in Mobile.

According to letters and diaries written by Barnsley, it was while spending those leisurely evenings at Woodlands that he began to feel the overwhelming presence of his beloved Julia. It was one evening in the parterre, as Barnsley sat gazing into the dark rippling waters of the garden pool that he believed he saw a perfect reflection of his Julia forming in the water. According to Barnsley, as the evenings passed she began to appear in various places throughout the gardens. Being so intrigued by the experience, he soon began gathering up all the material he could find on the subject of spirit communication. He also began corresponding regularly with the Sagers back in Mobile, about matters pertaining to life after death. Shortly thereafter, letters began pouring in from spiritual informants around the country who urged him to continue investigating his powers of communication. Barnsley was totally stunned to find that one of the letters had been written and signed by his deceased father-in-law, William Scarborough II, in which he described in detail the spiritual condition of his daughter, Julia Scarborough Barnsley.

As the days passed, according to Godfrey, Julia appeared more frequently, until eventually, he was able to communicate with her. Barnsley later stated that he regularly walked and talked with his Julia in the gardens and it was then, she informed him of her desire to have the mansion completed. As time progressed, Godfrey in his lonely state of mind, continued to spend many of his evenings near the fountain in the parterre, relaxing in the shadows of his beloved Julia.

He soon confided in his close friend, William Duncan, that he felt he had been blessed with some supernatural ability, perhaps even possessing the power of a "medium." But Duncan soon wrote to Barnsley, advising him to stay clear of the matter:

> *"You say you have a long letter about your attendant…from whom? Do let me advise you to*

have nothing more to do with him...Dismiss it from
your mind. You are not yet possessed. But this I
know, read the Bible and study...Prayer and faith
in the Lord Jesus Christ will overcome him and
all his machinations. God grant that you may soon
obtain the victory."

Barnsley did temporarily refrain from the practice, but after being so inspired by his new relationship with Julia, along with continued visits by Mrs. Berrien, he showed at the time he could not completely put the matter aside. Fully believing that the dead would return to the places they loved in life, and feeling that Julia was with him constantly, Barnsley seemed to have a new zest on life. He was suddenly filled with renewed vigor to finish the castle for his Julia. He immediately commissioned his overseer to have 300,000 bricks burned, to resume construction on the great manor and according to Barnsley, it was his deceased Julia that would select the rich furnishings for the final decorating of the house.

Some years later, Barnsley's wood craftsman, Robert Freeman and his workers, who installed the extensive woodwork in the great manor, handed down the following story:

"When we were working on the big house, some
mornings Mr. Barnsley would come by and say,
Miss Julia wanted something done such-and-
such-a-way. We didn't know what to think, with
her being dead and all, but we just did what he
said and kept on working."

When construction was resumed, Barnsley spared no expense in building his sixteen-room Italinate style manor house. Although it would be a number of years before the house would be inhabited, some of the great walls were soon erected and a roof was completed, over the structure, so that Barnsley finally had a place to put many of his furnishings that had been stored away in Savannah. He soon arranged for an entire trainload of the items, including a large French landau carriage to be brought to Kingston station. At Kingston, he had maintained a small stockyard of huge oxen and work mules that were capable of transporting the heavy loads on to Woodlands. For many years thereafter, early residents of the area would remember the excitement of Barnsley's trains arriving at Kingston station. One lady had stated:

"It looked as though a circus had come to the wilderness."

Drawing of Early Kingston
(Sketch by C.E.F. Hillen)

The late 1840's proved to be progressive years at Woodlands, as Barnsley continued to direct his overseer and workers toward the building of the estate. But after realizing that his children sometimes became lonely in the wilderness, he began to arrange some social functions at Woodlands, and with the Howards at Spring Bank, and also with the Stiles family at Stilesboro, Georgia about twelve miles from Woodlands. He brought in a tutor, a Mr. Burnam, from Mobile, for his younger sons, George and Lucien, and sent his older son Harold to Mr. Green's private school for boys, in Jamaica Plains, near Boston. Julia and Adelaide once again returned to C.W. Howard's school at Spring Bank. The eldest daughter, Anna, remained at Woodlands to care for Mother Scarborough who by this time, had began to suffer from a mental disorder. Mrs. Scarborough was soon returned to Savannah to live in an apartment with her son Joseph, where she would remain until her death. Within a few years, Godfrey's vindictive sister-in-law, Charlotte Taylor, found the upkeep of Scarborough Castle to be more than she could bear and the house was sold at a great loss.

During the 1840's, however, it was problems outside of Barnsley's household that affected his welfare. The Mexican War and the disturbance over the Oregon Treaty of 1846 had left the cotton market rather unstable, thus demanding more of Barnsley's attention at his seaport offices in New Orleans and Mobile. His attention was also diverted to the severe potato famine that had struck Ireland. His Irish overseer, John Connolly, had wrote to Barnsley in Mobile, requesting that he see to the passage of his brother and sister from Ireland to Georgia." He wrote:

"Ireland is a hotbed of pestilence and starvation! I beg of you to arrange their passage to this country."

A few months later, Connolly's family was transported to New Orleans on one of Barnsley's ships. It seemed that Barnsley was deeply touched by the extreme desecration of Ireland, for it was only a short time later that he arranged for several other Irish families and orphans to be brought to Woodlands. There they would assist John Connolly as special servants, and would care for various farming operations on the vast estate. As the years passed, Barnsley would prove to have a larger number of white "Irish" servants over Blacks. Most of the Irish immigrants would serve him well, and some of their descendants would remain in the area for generations to come.

When Barnsley found it necessary to make a trip from Woodlands to New Orleans in 1849, he decided to take his daughter Anna along with him, since she had been confined to the homestead for some time. Anna enjoyed the gaiety of the city while attending balls and parties with her father and his associates. It was there, she met her father's friend, Thomas C. Gilmour, originally from England who was a member of a prominent New Orleans shipping firm. A courtship soon evolved, and later Barnsley consented to their marriage that took place in New Orleans on February 25, 1850. Knowing that the building of his mansion for Julia was progressing rapidly, and feeling that his eldest daughter had married well, Barnsley now seemed more content than any time since his wife's death.

Anna and her husband spent the summer at Woodlands and then sailed for England where they settled down in Gilmour's home near London. In December of 1850, Anna gave birth to a son, Murray Barnsley Gilmour, and Godfrey Barnsley became a grandfather at the age of forty-five. The Gilmour's also became the parents of a daughter, Julia, in 1852.

Anna Barnsley Gilmour
in later years

CHAPTER 7

COMPLETING THE DREAM

The beginning of the 1850's seemed to bring much prosperity not only to Woodlands, but to the entire South as a whole. The cotton crops had increased greatly and the mills had expanded their operations, so that both factors and shippers benefited accordingly. Cass County in the North Georgia wilderness was also progressing with the rest of the south. More settlers had begun to move into the territory, and although the county was only eighteen years old, its population for 1850 had grown to 13,300 residents. There were 1712 houses, 601 farms and 3008 slaves. The county's property value, personal and real, was estimated to be $3,715,000.

After the railroad had been completed to Kingston on December 27, 1845, a network of rail lines was soon completed throughout the county. A group of local businessmen soon invested in a rail line to run from Kingston, fifteen miles west into Rome, Georgia. In 1847-48, the Western & Atlantic Railroad laid track from Kingston, north, through Spring Bank, Halls Mill, (three miles from Woodlands) and on to Adair Village, an old Indian settlement about twelve miles north of Kingston. The residents there soon moved their small hamlet to be near the railroad and began building a train station. In 1854, the community would be incorporated as "Adairsville, Georgia."

(Author's note: The original depot, completed about 1850, still stands at Adairsville.)

Early Adairsville, sketched by HARPERS WEEKLY newspaper

In 1851, another settlement was built along the railroad near Spring Bank, known as Cement, Georgia. It was there, C.W. Howard and his son-in-law, George Waring, had established the first hydraulic cement company in the state. Godfrey Barnsley later bought cement products from the company for thirty cents a bushel. By 1852, The Western & Atlantic Railroad had been extended sixty miles north through Calhoun, Dalton, and Ringgold, until reaching Chattanooga, Tennessee.

C.W. Howard's lime mill at Cement, GA, (late 1800's)

By this time, the new settlers of Cass County saw the urgent need for a better means of transportation through the wilderness. Barnsley therefore joined forces with his farm neighbor's, C.W. Howard, R.N. Kerr, Peyton Morrow, Robert Hood and Wesley Sutton, to rebuild the old Cherokee trails into broader and more substantial roadways. A short time later, Barnsley requested his friend, W.H. Stiles, at the House of Representatives, who was also director of post roads and post offices, to establish a post station at nearby "Spring Bank" and a small station at Woodlands. Once a better road had been constructed, and properly fenced off, as to prevent animals from obstructing its passage, the U.S. Mail stage began passing through Godfrey Barnsley's Woodlands.

A large brick building, sixty feet in length was erected near the main stage road, to serve as the overseer's quarters, a coach house, and the Woodlands Post Office. The estate was soon listed on the maps of the day, as Woodlands, Georgia. Barnsley's close friend, William Duncan, wrote from Savannah:

> *"I am sending you a new map of Georgia, and you will see "Woodlands" there, as large as life!"*

(Author's note: For a century and a half, the original mail room has remained at Woodlands.)

Godfrey Barnsley now had much reason to rejoice over the growth of Cass County and its new railroads, since it provided his estate much better access to the outside world.

By 1851, he had curtailed his trips abroad, preferring to leave that part of his business to other members of his firm, John Gardner of New Orleans and Edmund Sager in Mobile. It would also permit him to spend more time in directing the construction of his North Georgia estate.

Barnsley's personal business books for the year of 1851,

showed his net income, from commissions alone, to be $58,000. Much of the money he earned that year would be spent on special furnishings and additional work on his manor house and gardens.

FINAL CONSTRUCTION

It was during the decade of the 1850's that Godfrey's dream for his beloved Julia truly became a reality. As early as 1852, the huge manor and gardens, although still under construction, had become the central feature of "Woodlands." Since Barnsley was a true disciple of Andrew Jackson Downing, he had continued to follow a course distinctly outside the prevailing fashion in the south, and particularly in Georgia, in constructing his castle. In one letter, he had referred to it as his "Grand Italian Villa." The great manor, or villa, with its huge brick arches, porticos, and rambling terraces, featured sixteen rooms, and the main part of the house was in two stories.

The grand front entrance to the structure was a mammoth three story campanile or tower, that stood boldly overlooking thirty acres of landscaped grounds in which the workmen had begun to set out an array of ornamental trees and plants. The second floor of the campanile was designed as Godfrey's office, while the third story area provided a special sitting room, or overlook, that would allow Barnsley an elevated view of his vast domain.

By this time, Barnsley had shipped the majority of his valuable collections from Savannah to the up-country. He had also continued to collect additional furnishings and materials, from New York, Boston, Philadelphia, and various parts of Europe, to be installed at Woodlands, so that the interior fixtures of the great manor were truly magnificent. Black, white and pink marble imported from Italy and France, bordered the huge brick arches on the interior, and the fire mantles throughout the expansive structure were made of the same. Unique hand crafted doors and windows made of virgin pine, redwood, and cypress, were secured with sterling silver latches. On one end of the spacious entrance foyer was a large walk-in vault to protect Barnsley's currency, business documents, and his valuable collection of sterling silver.

It was while sketching the final plans, that Barnsley added a new feature to the manor, that was extremely outstanding for the day and age, especially in the Georgia wilderness; water closets of a very intricate design were added to both the first and second floors of the house. On one end of the huge structure, the roof had been designed to support a three hundred-gallon water storage tank to which water was forced from a spring-fed bog pond, in the deep valley to the south. At one end of the bog was a waterfall, beneath which was placed a newly designed hydraulic "ram" pump Barnsley had imported from Europe. The ram operated by the simple principle of natural force. As the weight of the water, from the fall, activated a valve on the pump, the cylinder of the ram turned perpetually, thus forcing water through a series of lead pipes up the hill to a large storage tank above the house. At that position, the water was simply gravity fed, by pulling a chain, or lever, to fill the various fixtures in the closets.

Another series of pipes were plumbed from the tank, to small outlets in the chimneys of the bedrooms, so that the winter fires heated the pipes, thus providing hot water to each of the bedrooms during the winter season. Also, a large pipe was plumbed from the storage tank out to the huge marble fountain in the boxwood parterre. By such an arrangement, the Barnsley Manor featured modern plumbing, with running hot and cold water, including enormous bathtubs with brass fixtures, inlaid marble vanities, and flushing commodes, even before the Civil War.

A specially hand carved staircase was installed on the north side foyer, directly across from the main drawing room, that gave entrance to the second story of the house. From the side foyer, a covered walkway led to the front entrance of the kitchen wing with its own dining room and billiard room, and filled with its own valuable antiquities. The huge stove Barnsley had imported from Liverpool, England, was built into one wall of the kitchen wing. It featured two large built-in ovens, produced its own hot water and a free running meat rotisserie that was powered by the natural draft of air flowing through the chimney. The stove was designed to accommodate one hundred and fifty people. Just beyond the stove, a broad flight of stairs lowered to a full basement that was designed as a wine and brandy cellar. According to his inventory ledger from the year 1851, he had already stored there some twenty-four hundred bottles of vintage wines and brandies. Much of the product was made by Barnsley himself, since he had already erected a large brandy still near one of the deep springs in the valley to the south. He had also begun to ferment a variety of wines from his own vineyards.

Nestled on the hillside a few yards below the brandy cellar was the coach house, post office, and the overseer's quarters. It was a long brick structure that stood overlooking the Woodlands village compound; a large complex of both wood and brick cottages, and other buildings fronting both sides of the main stage road. Many of Barnsley's collections and rare pieces of statuary were now stored in the compound. By this time, "Woodlands" had become a familiar village and stagecoach stop on the old Cherokee road winding through Cass County.

By late 1858, Godfrey's grand villa was so near completion that the family began to take up residence in the large structure. Although there was still much to be done, the huge mansion with its extensive left and right wings, provided an elegant twenty-six-room residence for the Barnsleys and their house servants.

The Unique Barnsley Stove
(Photo 1950's)

The unique furnishings throughout the entire complex were elaborate and costly to say the least. Among the collections were: Persian silk shawls, intricately inlaid tables, over five hundred pieces of fine china, a series of carved ivory plaques, and a fine collection of venetian glass. In the main entrance foyer stood an extraordinary gold clock originally from the Tuilleries in Paris. In the master's room was an enormous bed that had belonged to Louis XIV, and another bed of wrought iron, with matching chairs, that had been a gift to Barnsley from a Norwegian King. Standing in the center of the spacious drawing room, was a marble center piece, hand crafted by Italian monks in the eighteenth century, and a huge tranquil mirror from France covered one complete wall. The dining parlor in the kitchen wing featured a massive table that could seat forty guests, and a rare, mahogany sideboard, formerly owned by the Emperor of Brazil, Dom Pedro. Throughout the entire edifice, Barnsley had placed numerous statues of varied mold, made from bronze, marble, silver, ebony, and wood, along with one figure of a Roman gladiator trimmed in solid gold. Included among one of the collections, were custom made perfume bottles, a broach, and a large golden clock, that had originally belonged to her Majesty the Queen, Marie Antoinette of France.

Godfrey Barnsley had also acquired a valuable art collection consisting of several hundred rare paintings and tapestries, including a large portrait of Napoleon Bonaparte, that the famous Emperor had personally autographed.

In addition to these, were several collections of sterling silver and literally hundreds of other items too numerous to mention. George Barnsley soon sketched a drawing of the grand setting.

**Barnsley's Granddaughter with the
Queen Marie Antoinette Clock**

(Photo 1930's)

Drawing of Godfrey's Grand Villa

(By George Barnsley - 1858)

The landscaped grounds and gardens at Woodlands were no less spectacular than the grand manor itself. Since the first railroads were completed into the area, Barnsley had continued to transport many rare trees and shrubs to his Cass County Estate. Some of the trees were purchased from nurseries in New England and from P.J. Berckmans Fruitland Nurseries of Augusta, Georgia, while many others were being collected from the four corners of the world. Such a lavish decision of Barnsley's, however, proved to be quite a laborious and expensive task, since many of the aged trees were very large and difficult to transport. The foreign plants were usually shipped to the seaports on Barnsley's vessels, then thoroughly watered, and loaded onto railroad cars, to be shipped to Kingston, and Halls Mill, near Woodlands. Several ox drawn wagons were then connected to support each tree while transporting it over the last few miles to Woodlands. Once they arrived, Barnsley had only horse and oxen power, along with crude hand made trellises he had devised, to erect the massive trees, a miraculous achievement for the day and age. Listed among the many varieties were aged cedars of Lebanon, cunninghemias from Southeast Asia, yews from Ireland, firs from Scandinavia, a type of redwood from California, the Osage orange, and a wide variety of oaks and lindens from New England.

By the end of the last decade before the Civil War, the grounds and gardens at Woodlands were beginning to feature some of the rarest trees and shrubbery found in any part of the world.

(Author's note: An original Asian cunninghemia that Godfrey had set out in 1859, still stands in front of Barnsley Manor.)

Barnsley Manor (1880's)

Lying directly in front of the tower of the great manor was the massive boxwood parterre, complete with its own fountain and pool. The parterre had been geometrically designed with serpentine walks, winding through large border beds, that featured Italianate marble statuary, and overflowed with rich masses of brilliant plants. A large fountain of white marble, imported from Italy, was later erected over a circular pool basin in the center of the parterre.

The border beds contained Barnsley's own rare roses, grafted from Celtic stock, along with Madonna lilies, violets, hollyhock, Canterbury bells, fox glove, poppy verbena, tulips and British yews to name only a few.

Eventually, more than one hundred varieties of the rose were featured throughout the various gardens, with the rare "green rose" becoming a sort of symbol or trademark of the fabulous rose collection at Woodlands. The green rose of Woodlands would be embroidered into the silk dinner napkins, and printed on the fine Barnsley china.

A Gathering at the Manor (1880's)

Hosts of parties, weddings, and social functions were soon held at Woodlands. The Barnsley's lavishly entertained both local and foreign associates at the Grand Manor. Noted authors, artists, lawmakers and foreign ministers of trade were included among their guests.

see next page ➔

83

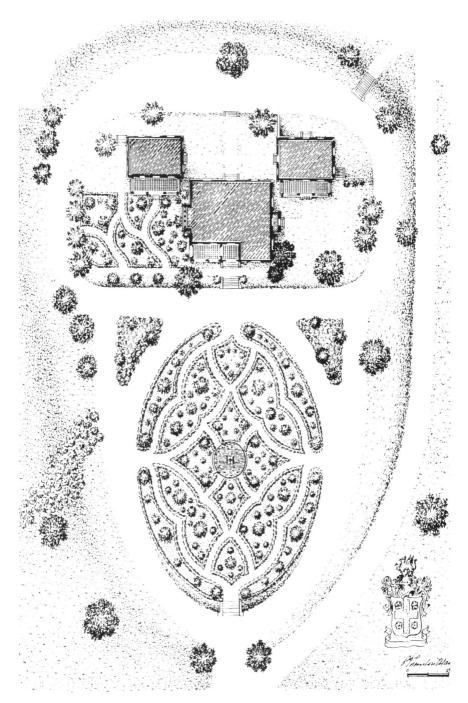

*Original grafted design of boxwood parterre
at Woodlands*

Early photo of a wedding in the parterre

The formal Boxwood "Parterre," featuring inlaid serpentine walks, imported marble statuary, and hundreds of rare plants and shrubs soon became a favorite site for weddings. The Barnsley's also spent many of their leisure hours relaxing in the beautiful parterre.

see next page ➔

Original Fountain

The parterre (1889)
(with a portion of fountain removed)

The cottage (about 1915)

Front View of Kitchen Wing (late 1800's)

To the south of the grand manor was a smaller, secondary parterre, lying perfectly formed in front of the left wing "new house" that had now become a guest cottage. Just below the front terrace between the parterres were the rockery gardens, filled with exotic plants and marble statuary, once again, remaining in true harmony with the unique concepts of Andrew Jackson Downing. To the rear of the manor, between the guest cottage and the kitchen wing, was the upper rose garden terrace, filled with its own collection of rare roses and wrought iron fixtures. Across the valley, facing a blue haze of mountain ridge to the west, were the lush fields of pasturage for the horses, cattle and sheep.

From the southern boundary view overlooking the deep valley below, one could see the bubbling waters of the great Indian spring that supplied the bog pond, and the bog gardens at the water cascade. A small green house (or cold frame) had been built into the hillside above the pond for the storage of special plants during the winter months. Standing about fifty yards beyond the water cascade, were the brandy stills and the oriental pond, utterly entrenched with excellent varieties of exquisite water plants. In a broad glade, on beyond the ponds, was featured one of the finest exhibits of rhododendrons in the south. Then, at the far end of the glade, stood the tall iron gates leading into "Deer Park," an area where Barnsley had intended to support a menagerie of animals. He had already placed in the park, a variety of reindeer, gazelle, llamas, English grass hogs and a pair of mountain goats.

Directly opposite Deer Park, rambling over the ledges and hillsides to the north of the great house, were the vast orchards and vineyards that eventually blended into the awesome beauty of the Appalachian Mountains in the distance.

In another direction, northeast of the prominent hill, stood Wolf Cave Mountain, with its massive fields of wheat, corn and rye.

Then finally, approaching from the front road gates, a quarter of a mile east of the formal setting came an impressive carriage drive flanked by tremendous hemlocks, lindens, cedars of Lebanon and the Osage orange. The broad drive had been divided to sweep around either side of the manor edifice, and continued to spiral downward, past the village compound, until finally reaching the spring house, at the lower guard gates, that featured its own gardens. The spring garden with its benches and tables, deeply shaded beneath clusters of huge oaks, provided a cool rest heaven for the Barnsley servants, and for stage coach travelers, during the hot summer months.

Imbedded into the hillside, above the spring house, was a broad flight of grand steps rising a full hundred yards, to the peak of the prominent hill, and to the entrance of Barnsley's Great Villa.

Toward the end of the 1850's, Godfrey Barnsley's fabulous Woodlands that engulfed more than four thousand acres, (and several thousand more in which he owned partnership or held options upon) was truly turning into a wilderness Eden.

Although there was still much more Barnsley had intended to accomplish, including the installation of a spiral staircase and applying stucco to the exterior of the great manor, Woodlands already contained a prominent mountain, and was considered a grand showcase of the South. From the tower of the great manor, the opulent view provided an immense framework of the beautiful Georgia wilderness as far as the eye could reach. Travelers would often drive their carriages out the main road through the wilderness to park near the prominent hill and have their picnics, while viewing the magnificent setting in the distance.

(Author's note: From an interview held in 1958 with Mrs. Fannie Colston (1874-1971) came the following:

> *"I remember riding in a buggy over the main Barnsley road through those woods, and passing those long pretty fields; until suddenly, there it was. The big castle high on the hill, and all the beautiful color surrounding the place. It was just marvelous. Folks came from every where just to see the place."*)

A distant view of the manor
(About 1880)

*Barnsley's Grand Estate beautifully
isolated in the wooded hills of the Georgia up-country truly
became a wilderness Eden. Travelers came from near and
far to view the huge "Villa" with its modern fixtures and
exotic gardens.*

see next page ➔

Godfrey had truly lavished a fortune on his Woodlands estate, a home in which his family and servants could indeed be proud. By the late 1850's, however, the family situation at the homestead had proved to be quite unsettled.

First of all, the tragedy that stalked Woodlands during the 1840's did not fail to return the following decade. In 1857, Barnsley's daughter, Adelaide, who was called "Lala," had married John K. Reid of New Orleans, and the couple soon moved to Ireland where Reid would represent the shipping firm of G. Barnsley & Co. But Adelaide soon became homesick and wanted to return to Woodlands. Her wish was finally granted, and she was returned to the homestead in time to give birth to a son, that she named "Godfrey Forrest Reid." But the long and rugged sea voyage from Ireland had weakened her considerably and she began to suffer from complications of childbirth. Adelaide died on October 2, 1858, and was buried in the small family cemetery at Woodlands, leaving her newborn son to be reared by her younger sister, Julia. Barnsley was deeply shocked over the death of his daughter, but was naturally very proud of his first grandchild to be born at Woodlands.

Adelaide Barnsley Reid

On the other hand, Barnsley's relationship with his son, Harold, had proven to be somewhat strained throughout the 1850's. He had naturally seemed to expect more from his eldest son, who although quite intelligent, had seemed to have a problem finding his real niche in life. After returning home from school in Boston, and then going on a rambunctious excursion to California, and back to Woodlands, he was sent to Barnsley's Mobile office to be apprenticed as a clerk. Harold was immediately attracted to the glittering life-style on Mobile Bay, and soon indulged himself in the gala activities of the waterfront, sometimes even at the expense of his father's business. It was due to an act of negligence, that Harold was responsible for a substantial loss to Barnsley's firm at Mobile. Godfrey wrote immediately:

"I am astounded at your culpable negligence which lost the company $3000. It shows only too plainly you do not pay attention to your duties."

A stern Barnsley chastised Harold by sending him back to Woodlands to be tutored at farm work under his overseer, John Connolly. But Harold became bored with life in the country, and his love for the sea soon lured him to New Orleans, where he again worked for his father under the strong discipline of the company clerk, Mr. Jay Norman. In a short time, however, Harold decided he would never realize his own worth by remaining in his father's business, and left New Orleans rather suddenly. In a letter of explanation to his father dated August 15, 1854, he had written:

"My intention is to drink no more, and avoid women as much as possible. My mind is made up and I will win the golden prize or never return. I will never stain the name of Barnsley, as I will change my name as soon as I engage in any business you wouldn't approve."

Within a year and a half, Harold had written again stating that he had planned to become a sea captain and would reside in the Orient. But at first it seemed that Barnsley was so disturbed over his actions, that he had refused to answer his letters. Harold soon wrote again from his new home in Hong Kong:

"If it is the intention of all of you to have nothing more to do with me, let me know, and the name Barnsley will be extinct as far as I am concerned. You will never hear from me again! Please write!"

After feeling some remorse, Barnsley finally wrote to Harold concerning his departure:

"As I am not a believer in chance, but in an overruling providence, I have concluded it was for the best. The reasons that you stated for leaving so abruptly, seem to me insufficient, but young people judge differently from old ones and I will not discuss the point. But I must say, there is only a certain portion of happiness attainable in this world, and none is exempt from cares and trials. The profession you have chosen is one of toil and danger. But I hope you will do your duty at all times to conduct yourself as a Christian gentleman. Remember that all human actions will determine the results and if mankind will do wrong they bring on themselves the inevitable consequences of a violation of moral law. Do not omit reading the Bible! I am hoping you will write often, and with the assurance that you are constantly remembered in our prayers to the supreme ruler of all things, I remain your affectionate father."

After 1857, Barnsley received several letters from Harold, describing his new shipping business in Hong Kong. But the correspondence came to an abrupt halt, after a letter was received on July 4, 1859. Several months later, Barnsley wrote to the head of the British garrison in Hong Kong, General G.J. Kenan, requesting help concerning the whereabouts of his son. As the months passed, he spent a considerable sum of money with investigators in search of Harold, but with no results.

After finally going through another year of frustrating suspense over his son's disappearance, Barnsley received word that Harold's ship had been taken over by pirates in the South China Sea, and he had been shot while trying to swim to safety. But Barnsley was never furnished positive evidence of such, and for the rest of his days he would be plagued by the haunting mystery; a mystery that would remain at Woodlands forever.

George Barnsley later wrote in his memoirs concerning the disappearance of his brother, Harold:

> *Harry never came back from across the sea; would he never tire of those horrid Chinese! How often as the sun's last lingering rays rested on the roses, have I glanced toward the gate half-hoping to see him come...my poor brother, Harry...thou too gone...thy spirit, brother, dwells with us; thy voice still echoes and thy name is still dear as when we sported together in childhood...*

Meanwhile, Barnsley had sent his youngest son, Lucien, to his New Orleans office, to be apprenticed in the business of cotton, since he had hoped that at least one of his sons would be pronged to follow in his footsteps. In order to keep up with the growing demand on cotton for foreign markets, Barnsley had taken two new associates into his company who were ship owners from Northern Germany. The Baron's Henry Von Schwartz and his son, Charles, who had recently engaged their ships in the foreign cotton trade, proved to be an asset to Barnsley's firm. Lucien seemed to learn well, working with the Von Schwartz father and son team who would prove to be lifelong friends of the Barnsleys.

After the death of Adelaide, and with Anna living in England, Julia was the only Barnsley daughter residing at Woodlands. After finishing C.W. Howard's school at Spring Bank, she had entered Montpelier College near Macon, where she had received a grade of excellence for all her work. By the age of eighteen, she had mastered three foreign languages, and was presented with a note of "correct and ladylike for all her conduct." Her schoolmaster wrote to Barnsley:

> *"She will return to you all that a Christian father could reasonably desire."*

Julia had also grown to love and respect the family homestead, spending many of her hours in the formal gardens where Godfrey and his Julia had often strolled, or riding her favorite horse across the rolling hills of her father's fabulous Woodlands. Julia was determined to remain at Woodlands to rear her sister's child, and to assist her father in maintaining the Barnsley household.

It was in 1854, that Barnsley's son, George, had entered Oglethorpe University at Midway, Georgia, where he had first studied theology, and then medical science. After completing his studies there in 1857, he had hoped to eventually practice medicine. But it was George who would become the next overseer of his father's estate.

After suffering a substantial loss from a financial panic in 1857, Barnsley had returned from New Orleans and decided that several things were out of order at Woodlands. On finding that certain work had not been completed on the manor, and that some of the valuable brandy was missing from the cellar, and unaccounted for, a stressed Barnsley suddenly accused John Connolly of mismanaging funds and neglecting his duties. Connolly, who had served the estate for sixteen years, was so disturbed over Barnsley's actions that he immediately left Woodlands. A few months later, Barnsley placed his son, George, in charge of the family estate.

(Author's note: Although Godfrey Barnsley had been known to spend large sums of money on his family and estate, he was also considered to be extremely conservative. Even when his mind was fully occupied with business affairs, he would often write from foreign ports, admonishing his family and workers to be thrifty and conserve while running the estate and to make sure everything was accounted for, down to the minute detail. Barnsley had in fact required his son George to keep a daily journal of his activities while operating Woodlands.)

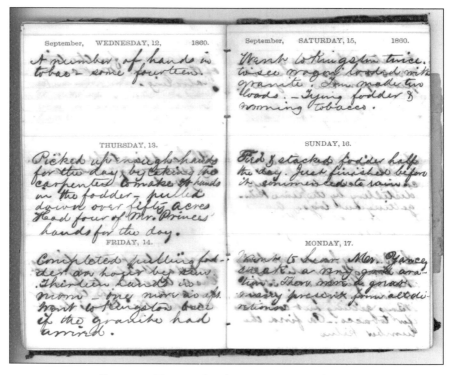

George Barnsley's Journal of 1860

Godfrey's strong conservatism again surfaced in a letter dated November 16, 1860, to his son, George, at Woodlands:

"You do not study economy, and I am afraid you never will. I informed you that you could use $100 to buy more hogs. But now I learn you have taken $55 from the account, and eighty odd dollars, making upwards of $35 above the amount. You have gone in opposition to my advice, and also of common sense, and now, you say you are in need of more money. I do not know what to make of your movements. You will have to turn over a new leaf."

It also became evident that Barnsley was constantly mindful of the designing, financing, and building of his grand villa. Although much of his life was consumed by his foreign travels, he continually wrote to the overseer and workers at Woodlands concerning the intricate details of construction. On December 13, 1859, he had written:

"I am afraid you and Edward have made sad work in digging out the gutter on the north side. If I recollect rightly, a fall of 2 3/4 inches would be enough. The distance from the front is about 50 feet, and a fall of one inch in 15 feet would be plenty to carry the water. And the joists are 11 inches, leaving 7 inches which would be plenty without iron supports. Also, if the scaffolding be sound about the house, it should be allowed to remain in case we are able to cement the outside this summer. – You must study the sketches I have enclosed."

By 1860, Barnsley was spending much of his time at Woodlands, in the company of his daughter, Julia, his son, George, and grandson, Godfrey Forrest Reid, and was continuing to beautify his estate whenever possible. Though rumors were brewing of a severe national conflict, he was beginning to enjoy a new prosperity that seemed to reign throughout the South.

The state of Georgia was growing rapidly, with thirty-two new counties being formed in the last decade before the Civil War. Foundries, yarn mills, tanneries, and many other facilities were beginning to appear throughout the state. But its economy had definitely depended on slavery, because Georgia was the leading state of the slavery south. In 1860, her property in Negroes was worth more than all her cities and land combined. But Barnsley still believed it was better to hire laborers or domestic servants whenever possible. Since he had acquired a large staff of Irish servants and farmers, along with hiring slave workers from other owners, he only paid taxes on six slaves that he legally owned in 1859. A few years earlier, he had attempted to purchase or lease some additional slaves that were skilled in construction work, but found they were too expensive and decided against it.

Barnsley had also preferred to stay clear of politics as much as possible, although he had begun to keep a watchful eye on the political affairs of Georgia and the United States throughout 1860. He knew that any turmoil brewing inside the country would certainly cause a disturbance in the cotton trade, and from what he had been observing, he felt that a dissolution of ties binding the states was something very certain, and not far distant.

CHAPTER 8

THE WAR BETWEEN THE STATES

When the Great War finally erupted between North and South, on April 12, 1861, Godfrey Barnsley was determined to remain neutral in the conflict. He had after all, remained a British subject and was also an international sea merchant who had friends and associates in both the North and South.

Since cotton had represented a large percentage of Great Britain's economy, Barnsley was convinced that his "Mother England" would enter the conflict on the side of the South, and the war would be short lived. He fully agreed with John Pepper, an associate in New Orleans, who wrote on June 2, 1861:

"Great Britain will insist on a steady supply of cotton and we can fully expect her as an ally very soon!"

Barnsley also felt certain that the war would cause a rapid rise in the price of cotton in Europe and the southern economy would remain strong and profitable. Although he still professed his neutrality, he soon invested a total of $81,500, in confederate bonds, feeling sure it would earn him even greater profits. But he would eventually come to regret such an investment.

Although Barnsley had advised his family to remain

neutral, and not to get involved with the politics of the war, his sons felt different about the matter. George was convinced the war would be long and costly, and felt he should take part in it to protect the homefront. He wrote to his brother, Lucien, who was still in New Orleans, on April 24, 1861:

> *"I have spoken to Pa in regard to our joining the navy, but he discourages the idea."*

A short time later, Lucien returned home, and without consulting any one, he and George went over to Rome, Georgia and enlisted as privates for three years in the "Rome Light Guards." They soon joined the rest of the young men, "caught up in the enthusiasm of the war," and were transported by train to Winchester, Virginia. Several years later, a roster of the men who served would show the following:

Muster roll of Company A, 8ᵗʰ Regiment
Georgia Volunteer Infantry
Army of Northern Virginia,
C. S. A. Floyd County Ga., (Rome Light Guards)

Barnsley, George S....Private May 18, 1861, appointed Hospital Steward December 24, 1862. Detailed in Medical Department at Richmond, Va., in 1864. Appointed Assistant Surgeon, March 22, 1865.

Barnsley, Lucien L....Private May 18, 1861. Detailed to report to Dr. Miller at Greensboro, Ga., October 31, 1864.

George Barnsley

Lucien Barnsley

On arriving in Virginia, the Barnsley brothers were surprised to find their father's Savannah attorney, Francis Bartow, also enlisted with the Northern Army of Virginia. Together they would soon participate in the first major battle of the war, known as the "First Battle of Manassas," or as referred to by Northerners as the "Battle of Bull Run," that took place on July 21, 1861. Although the engagement turned out to be a great victory for the South, Francis Bartow was mortally wounded in the field. George Barnsley later wrote that he and Lucien were together holding the banner when Col. Bartow went down.

A few months later, Georgia's Governor, Joseph E. Brown, announced that he intended to change the name of "Cass County," since it was originally named for Governor Lewis Cass of Michigan, an early surveyor of Cherokee Indian affairs, but also a Northerner, who was now sustaining a war on the people of the South. According to legend, Governor Brown had stated that no county in the state of Georgia should be named for a "damn Yankee"!

On hearing the news, Godfrey Barnsley, and his associates, C.W. Howard and W.H. Stiles, suggested to the governor that no better honor could be bestowed than to name the county for their friend and attorney, Francis Bartow, who had just lost his life at Manassas. Thus it was, on December 6, 1861, that old Cass, became known as Bartow County. It is also interesting to note that the town of "Cassville" was changed to Manassas, after the first Confederate victory, and remained under that name until the end of the war, when it was once again called Cassville.

During the summer of 1861, Barnsley returned to New Orleans to check the status of his business, only to discover the port was already blockaded by Union ships. The city had presented the appearance of a military camp, with federal soldiers at every corner. But Barnsley was still optimistic that the recent southern victory at "Manassas" would bring the recognition needed to make Great Britain intervene, and thus force a lifting of the blockades. There was some reason for rejoicing among Southerners, when in mid-September, the British steamer, "Bermuda," did slip through the blockades with a heavy cargo of supplies for the Confederacy. Boarded on the ship were 50,000 pairs of shoes, 24,000 blankets, twenty rifled canons, 7,000 infield rifles, 1,000,000 cartridges, 40,000 pounds of powder, and a quantity of pistols.

It was hoped the vessels would remain in the South, and join the Confederate Navy but such did not prove to be the case. By that time, Southern merchants were fully disappointed that the blockades of Southern ports had not brought on a more rapid intervention by Great Britain. But the South did see a rise in the price of cotton as Barnsley had expected.

For the first six months, two ships in his service, under the direction of the Baron Henry Von Schwartz, and his son, Charles, were able to break through the hastily established blockades, so that the company realized a profit of $60,000. It was also the Von Schwartz team that was later successful in smuggling a shipload of Confederate supplies through the Port of Nassau. It was by using a clever scheme of first sailing under the Confederate flag, and then hoisting the German flag when coming insight of the enemy, that they succeeded with the venture.

(Author's note: Both of these flags were eventually brought to Woodlands, where they remained until they were sold at an auction in 1942.)

Since Barnsley had remained one of the most active cotton factors of the South during the first year of the war, he decided to continue with business in spite of the blockades, hoping to ride out the tide until they could be lifted. But after the fall of New Orleans, The G. Barnsley & Company was forced to close its offices along the southern sea ports. In early 1862, Godfrey Barnsley returned to his North Georgia estate, where he would remain throughout the lonely days of the war. He kept close to his great manor and gardens and continued to improve and beautify the estate as much as his funds would permit.

It was in 1862, he ordered from P.J. Berckman's Fruitland Nurseries in Augusta, Georgia, a large order of flower bulbs and fruit trees that were later set out at Woodlands.

Fruitland Nurseries,

Augusta, Ga. Feb 13 1862

Mr Godfrey Barnsley

Bought of **P. J. BERCKMANS.**

6	Fushia $4 per 12 / 1 Duculea 50¢ 6 Pelargoniums 35¢	5 00
1	Heliotrope Voltaireanum 37½ 6 Azalea 3¢¢	2 62
2	Magnolia fuscata 50¢ / 1 Olea fragrans.	1 00
1	Taxus Elegantissima 2¢ / 1, Tardiva alpsuna	2 00
2	Araucaria Imbricata	2 00
1	Gardenia Radicans 37½ / 1 Washingtonia 50¢	87
1	Abies Mormuda 50¢ 2 Abies Excelsa 25¢	1 00
1	Picea Pictinata 25¢ 1 Fagus atropurpurea 37½	67
1	Cotoneaster 7¢ 2 Cupressus Ericoides 50¢	1 37
1	Sweet Pomegranate 25¢ 2 Figs 25¢	75
3	Standard peartrees 50¢	1 50
1	Dwarf Peach 25¢ 2 Dwarf peach trees	75
	Box	50
		$ 20 09
	Cash returned Prepayment	1 32
	P. J. Berckmans	$ 21 35

Exhibit 2—(a)

135

Barnsley's main association during the war was limited to his daughter, Julia, his Grandson, Godfrey Forrest Reid, and his loyal Irish housemaid, Mary Quinn. He only left his property occasionally, to visit the C.W. Howard and W.H. Stiles families, or to take brief trips in his French Landau carriage into the local towns of Adairsville, Kingston and Cassville, so that most people looked upon him as a wealthy recluse.

He became known as "The Rich Englishman" who had an extensive stock of whiskey and brandy for which the locals tried to beg or barter as much as possible. Barnsley was often amused at some of his country neighbors who would send for wine and brandy with the excuse, "it was the only way they could get their hired hands to work," or "a few bottles of port for a sick wife." After returning from New Orleans, he had expanded his distilling operations to produce more wine, peach brandy, and corn whiskey, that he felt would provide a source of income during the financially strained years of the war. When the Confederate army learned he was manufacturing such products, he was called upon to supply brandy to several Confederate posts throughout the South. The product was used by the army as an anesthesia and for cleansing purposes. On one occasion, he was given an order to ship one hundred and fifty gallons of solid peach brandy to a Confederate hospital in Vicksburg, Mississippi, for which he would be paid eight dollars per gallon, in Confederate bonds.

In 1862, Barnsley's close friend, Reverend C.W. Howard of "Spring Bank," suddenly announced that he was forming his own regiment to join the Confederate Army. Barnsley was totally shocked and had thought it absurd since Howard was almost fifty-two years of age, with no previous military experience. But Howard was determined to carry out his plan. A few months later, a large group of North Georgians joined Howard's 63rd Georgia regiment, and went off to fight in the war.

In the months to come, with many of the local men away at war, Barnsley found it necessary to handle a number of menial tasks for himself and his county neighbors. He was soon requested to care for the slave family of Reverend J. Jones, near Kingston, who had left with Howard's regiment, to fight in the war.

On one occasion, while traveling near Adairsville, he was disturbed to find a neighboring farm lady, whose husband was off to war, carrying a large sack of corn to a mill twelve miles away in order for her children to have bread. On returning home, he instructed his servants, Amos and Ned Phinizy, to keep all the "war widows" in the area supplied with free grain from Woodlands, for the remainder of the war. Barnsley usually kept an abundance of wheat that was known to be of excellent quality. According to a Bill of Lading in 1861, he had shipped two hundred bushels of fine grade wheat, by riverboat, from Rome, Georgia to Atlanta for a price of one dollar per bushel.

But as the days passed with no end of the war in sight, Barnsley's sources of income changed drastically, and he began to look for other "marketable" items on his estate. He continued to expand the farming operations, along with additional pasturage for cattle and sheep, and during the year of 1862, grew 2000 pounds of tobacco that he sold for $260.59. After receiving word that manufacturers in Rome and Atlanta were paying high prices for all the scrap metals available, Barnsley had the zinc sheets removed from the roofs of the carriage shed, and spring house, and replaced them with wood shingles. He then sold four hundred and fifty pounds of zinc metal to the "Noble Brothers Company" in Rome, Georgia, for fifty cents per pound. In January, 1863, he removed one hundred and thirty-five pounds of lead water pipes from the chimneys of the great manor, and sold them to the W.D. Smyth Company in Atlanta, for which he received one dollar per pound, in Confederate currency. The metals were needed to produce artillery for the Confederate army, and Barnsley was eager for the income it provided. He had a large number of servants and workers at Woodlands, dependent on his support, and that was no easy task in such critical times.

By the year of 1863, the village of Kingston, six miles south of Woodlands, had become the largest railroad junction in Northwest Georgia. Since Atlanta, with its mills and foundries had become the "warehouse" of the Confederacy, General Robert E. Lee's army of Virginia depended greatly on their supplies from Georgia, by way of the W & A Railroad through Kingston. And since the Commander-in-Chief of Union armies, Ulysses S. Grant, was already planning his strategy to invade Georgia, the Confederates soon established a military post at Kingston to properly maneuver men and supplies to defend Atlanta. Also, a Confederate arsenal was set up at Adairsville, twelve miles north of Kingston.

General Grant had believed that no peace could be activated until the military power of the Confederacy was completely broken. He therefore intended to penetrate as deeply as possible into the heart of Georgia, and to inflict all the damage he could to the rail line supplying the Confederate war resources. Thus it was that General Lee sent down Captain James P. Baltzelle, a provost Marshal from Minton, Virginia, to take charge of the important Confederate "hub" at Kingston, and keep the supply line open from Atlanta to Richmond.

Shortly after arriving at Kingston, the Captain heard about Barnsley's grand estate, and his enormous stock of brandy, and decided to pay the place a visit.

It was a pleasant Sunday afternoon, in the fall of 1863, when Captain Baltzelle first rode through the front gates into Godfrey Barnsley's Woodlands. He was immediately overtaken by the grandeur of the estate and later wrote in his memoirs that he was fully amazed to find such a magnificent setting lying in the heart of the wilderness. The Captain received a warm and friendly welcome from Barnsley and his daughter, Julia, who were of course, anxious to be updated on the latest events of the war. Captain Baltzelle seemed to fit well with the Barnsleys, for in the weeks to come he visited more frequently for Sunday dinners, long walks through the gardens, and sometimes to purchase a few gallons of Barnsley's brandy for the Confederate post at Kingston.

Godfrey Barnsley
(Courtesy of Michael Garland)

Daughter Julia
(From the Paintings of Bayard Cole)

Baltzelle, a lonely soldier far from home, was especially intrigued by his association with Barnsley's lovely daughter, Julia. He noted in his record book that Julia often entertained him by beautifully performing on her piano forte. And Julia would write in her diary, that on her first sight of the Captain, she was greatly impressed by the positive and cheerful nature of the dashing young officer. As the months passed, their friendship would ripe. into romance. After finding the Captain to be a gentleman of honor, Barnsley consented to the marriage of his daughter, Julia Bernard Barnsley, to Confederate Captain James Peter Baltzelle. The ceremony took place at Woodlands, Georgia on February 29, 1864.

George Barnsley, who had temporarily returned home from the war to recuperate from a case of typhoid, participated in the event. Writing in his journal of 1864, George described the wedding festivities:

"The wedding evening came at last, a day to be remembered in the history of Woodlands. My father, the dear old gentleman, is worn out from the troubles of war, and I am to receive the guests and prepare for them. Full instructions were given to the servants, and I was prepared to meet Captain C.W. Howard and family...a glowing fire in the library, and 'something warm and liquid' was on the table.

The parlor in the cottage looked so sweet and pretty. Captain Howard, in a soft, clear and solemn voice, read the service, and the 'twain were one'. Then the feast began. The table spanned the full length of the billiard room, in the kitchen wing. It was the most beautiful I had seen since the beginning of the war.

Everything went off well and the guests seemed to appreciate the good old wine. The tables were removed and the dancing began. At 2 a.m., the ladies retired, and later on the older members of the party, but the younger remained and beguiled the hours with song and joke until "Aurora" never fresher than we, drove by in her chariot of fire. To those guests who stayed, an ample breakfast was given and then the party dispersed. Everyone was happy through the long night and the servants were constantly on hand and cheerful."

The newlyweds enjoyed a rather simple honeymoon at Woodlands, and the Captain was soon transferred to a new post at Augusta, Georgia. Two months later, a whirlwind of Union armies came roaring through North Georgia.

THE ATLANTA CAMPAIGN

Northern victories at Gettysburg and Vicksburg had by this time reversed the course of the war, and the Confederates were soon forced to retreat into the mountains of North Georgia. In April of 1864, the Union Major General, William T. Sherman and his three major armies, consisting of more than 90,000 soldiers, launched their famous "Atlanta Campaign" against General Joseph E. Johnston's Confederate forces. Although Sherman's Union forces had outnumbered Johnston's almost two to one, Sherman did not by any means take Joe Johnston for granted. He knew very well, that "old Joe" was a brilliant well-seasoned soldier, who had built a strong disciplined army, and would be difficult to defeat. As a matter of fact, the two generals knew each other quite well, since they had spent their earlier years together as friends, while attending West Point Military Academy, in Ohio. But now, the two old friends were in the deep

South, blatantly sustaining a war against one another.

General Sherman's armies had been named for the three major rivers of the east, the Cumberland, the Ohio, and the Tennessee. He, and his headquarters staff traveled with 34,000 soldiers in the army of the Cumberland, commanded by General George Thomas. It was to be a holding force keeping the enemy in place, while his army of the Tennessee under General James B. McPherson, and the Ohio troops under General John M. Schofield were to swing around the sides and probe the confederate flanks in order to break their position guarding the railroad.

On May 15th, at Resaca, twenty miles north of the Barnsley estate, both sides fought hard for several hours, until Joe Johnston's Confederates were finally outflanked and forced to move farther south toward Calhoun and Adairsville, on the W & A Railroad line.

Heavy skirmishing was heard around Adairsville, on the morning of May 17th, as Johnston attempted to defend the state arsenal there. But when Sherman captured Adairsville, during the early morning hours of the 18th, old Joe had disappeared.

Early Adairsville with Original Depot

117

In an effort to find the quick maneuvering Johnston, Sherman's tactic was to form a broad pattern formation, at Adairsville, with Thomas' army in the center, following the railroad towards Kingston, and Scholfields's Ohio forces going east through Mostellers Mill to Cassville. Meanwhile, McPherson's army had been flanking the west, traveling through McGuires Crossing and Hermitage, just north of Rome, Georgia. It was McPherson's army that soon advanced toward Godfrey Barnsley's Woodlands.

THE WAR AT WOODLANDS

On the morning of May 18, 1864, Godfrey Barnsley sat beside Julia's fountain in the parterre, listening to the distant rumble of cannon fire that had been going on since early morning. According to the memoirs of the Irish housemaid, it was about a quarter of noon when the family servant, Uncle "Moses", came to alert Barnsley that all of the mountain ridges, surrounding Woodlands were covered with Union Soldiers.

Barnsley immediately ordered a younger servant to secure all the women and children into safe quarters. He had no sooner reached his grand villa until hundreds of Kenner Garrad's Union Calvary unit flooded the entire area around his home and gardens.

(Author's note: From an interview with Molly Curtis in 1959, who remembered the invasion as an eight-year-old child, came the following:

118

"Me and Mammy was lookin out the kitchen house window when the soldier mens hosses came jumpin over the fences and runnin every which way. And Mammy say, 'Looks like bad trouble, get on the floor child!' and I did! She was afraid they'd set fire to the house and so everybody went down to the cellar and stayed...and pretty soon we heard lots o'racket and fightin goin on down the hill there. Folks was hollering, and guns firin...and some got shot too. But they never did burn the place, so we went back up stairs with the rest, and I remember seeing all the soldier men. They was lots of them, and lots more of em kept coming down the roads. Some of them stayed on a while too, and they stole everything they could get they hands on, my mammy said. And when they finally left the place that whole valley down thah by the creek had all sorts of garbage and stuff lying everywhere. It was the worst mess I'd ever seen.")

According to official war records, it was evident that a triangle of significant events took place at Woodlands on that afternoon of May 18, 1864. First of all, as Kenner Garrad's Union Calvary was about to enter the Barnsley estate, the 2nd Alabama Light Calvary led by Confederate Colonel Richard Earle, (a friend to the Barnsleys), was successfully forcing a division of federals from Kingston back toward Woodlands, taking a number of prisoners. At about the same time 16,000 troops of General J.B. McPherson's Union army of the Tennessee were beginning to arrive on the mountain ridges surrounding Woodlands.

After discovering McPherson's army almost in their midst, Colonel Earle and his small band of Confederates began to hastily retreat back toward the Barnsley home, to warn the family of the oncoming invasion. On suddenly catching sight of Barnsley's housemaid, Mary Quinn, standing in the basement door of the kitchen wing, Earle gallantly charged the hill, yelling to her and the others to take cover and prepare for a possible enemy attack. Earle then headed back down the hill attempting to form a new position with his troops when he was suddenly confronted with enemy fire. It was then that Colonel Earle was shot and killed by a federal sharpshooter listed as: T.H. Bonner of Company "A" 98th Illinois Infantry Volunteers. A skirmish quickly erupted between the 2nd Alabama and the Advance Guard of McPherson's Army. But the Union forces, greatly outnumbering the 2nd Alabama, quickly forced the Confederates to withdraw, and the Federal soldiers soon occupied Woodlands.

A short time later, General McPherson arrived on the grounds and met Master Barnsley. After investigating the circumstances surrounding Colonel Earle, he granted Barnsley permission to bury his gallant friend on the rear rose garden terrace behind the great manor.

(Author's note: Still standing among the rambling roses at Barnsley Gardens, is a small confederate stone marking the grave of "Colonel Richard Earle" of the 2nd Alabama Calvary.)

Col. R.G. Earle
of Jacksonville, AL (1858)

Earle's Tombstone

*An artist's sketch of Woodlands
during Union Invasion*

*The short lived skirmish at Woodlands actually took place in
the lower valley to the west of the house. It seems however, the
sketch artist for the "Harper's Weekly" newspaper was intent
on showing the Grand Villa, and therefore placed the entire
conflict directly in front of the prominent setting.*

see next page →

HARPER'S WEEKLY.

A JOURNAL OF CIVILIZATION.

Vol. VIII.—No. 392]

NEW YORK, SATURDAY, JULY 2, 1864.

WOODLANDS, GEORGIA.

On arriving at Woodlands, General McPherson was immediately captivated with his findings: First of all, he was totally stunned to find that a British subject had erected such a fabulous European style estate in the wilds of North Georgia, highlighted by a large British flag waving gracefully from the tower of the manor, to show both his heritage and neutrality.

Secondly, the General was surprised to find that Barnsley's Negro servants were living a civilized and comfortable life-style, and had no desire to leave Woodlands, their beloved home.

McPherson was also overwhelmed by the awesome beauty of Woodlands and its gardens, as he remarked:

"This is a little piece of heaven itself, and I forbid it to be trampled by soldier or horse."

After having a brief conversation with Barnsley, who kindly requested his home be spared, the General agreed to protect the family residence and to set up his quarters in Barnsley's left wing "cottage." McPherson at once ordered guards to be placed around the various gardens to keep soldiers from destroying the beautiful grounds. They were allowed to forage only, to secure food supplies for themselves and their horses. Barnsley also remembered that McPherson warned his headquarters staff that "nothing should be destroyed or taken, as the property belongs to a British subject."

(Author's note: In reflecting on the life of General James B. McPherson, it was interesting to note that both sides had commonly referred to him as the "Gentleman Warrior," who had been known to protect civilians and private property wherever possible.)

General James Birdseye McPherson

Nevertheless, it was only a few hours after the general had issued his orders, that a small group of foragers secretly forced entry into the heavily stocked brandy cellar, beneath the kitchen wing. They soon helped themselves to over two thousand bottles of wine, brandy and imported scotch, and began secretly passing it around to others, so that several of the squadrons camped around the hill became drunk on the powerful brandy. While using the spirits to influence the guards, they secretly ransacked the upper kitchen wing, and the village compound, in the valley below, stealing or destroying many of Barnsley's valuable collections and statuary. The unruly soldiers soon broke into the farm storage buildings, wastefully slaughtering the livestock and taking, or destroying most of the wheat grain, tobacco, and farm implements. The rampage continued across the valley, throughout the night, while McPherson rested quietly in the cottage on Godfrey Barnsley's prominent hill.

General McPherson had sent and received several dispatches while camped at Woodlands, including the order to move on Kingston, to join General Sherman's army of the Cumberland, who had captured that city on the morning of May 19, 1864. It is most likely that General McPherson never realized the extent of his men's disobedience at Woodlands. For on the next morning, he paused on the front steps to bid Barnsley farewell, and ordered his commanding staff to walk carefully through the breathtaking gardens to view them, before departing for Kingston. Some of the soldiers remained for several hours after McPherson's departure, and continued to heavily ransack the estate.

After the army had left Woodlands, the Barnsley's were also plagued by various groups of stragglers, taking advantage of the spoils of war. On May 23, 1864, Barnsley sent a note to General Sweeny at Spring Bank to be passed on to McPherson at the Union headquarters in Kingston, requesting protection from the stragglers. It read, in part:

> *"Please provide me protection against the succession of marauding stragglers infecting my valley...a party of four has just left, stating that they belonged to Wiley's Brigade."*

Although Barnsley's friends had thought it a foolish pursuit to expect any protection from the Yankees, he had felt that McPherson was a gentleman and would consider his plea. Barnsley proved to be correct, for some days later, a Union Marshal arrived to post guard over Woodlands and remained there until the first of October.

It was also during the Union occupation of Woodlands that a most interesting and heroic event took place involving Barnsley's Irish housemaid, Mary Quinn. (From Mary's diary came the following story):

One morning, she had watched closely as one of the soldiers

approached Barnsley at the top of the stairs above the brandy cellar, asking him for the time of day. When Barnsley pulled out his gold pocket watch, the soldier suddenly jerked it from his hand and ran down the steps in an effort to escape through the brandy cellar. With fury in her eyes, Mary quickly sprang from the cook's room and chased the culprit into the cellar, although Barnsley had tried to stop her.

"No! No!...I'm sick of the dirty devils taking everything they want...but they'll not do anymore, long as I'm alive!" exclaimed Mary loudly.

On catching up with the soldier in the cellar, Mary gave him a good face clawing, demanding that he give back the watch. But the bloody-faced soldier knocked Mary to the floor with the butt of his rifle, then threatened to burn the house and escaped. After finally regaining some of her strength, Mary discovered a letter that had fallen from the Yank's pocket during the scuffle that revealed his name and rank.

With the letter still clutched in her hand, Mary headed immediately to McPherson's quarters, angrily screaming her way through the guards until the General agreed to see her. After reminding him that he had promised to protect the people of Woodlands, McPherson agreed to investigate her story and sent for the company to which the man belonged.

"Can you also identify this thief and woman beater?" asked the General.

"Oh, that I can!" said Mary. "And he will be marked good where I scratched him, he will!

After a lineup, Mary quickly identified the scar-faced soldier, and McPherson ordered him to give her back the watch. According to Mary's diary, the General was quoted,

"A man that strikes a woman is not fit to be my soldier…Should I have him shot?

126

"Oh no," said Mary, "I don't want any more of his dirty blood on me hands, than I already have there."

The General remarked, "Well, then, I shall send this scoundrel to Chattanooga in ball and chain, to work on the fortifications till the war is over." The General laughed when Mary described him as being a gentleman, but in low company. "I think we had better enlist you," said the General.

(Author's note: A few years later, a tumor developed on Mary's body, directly where she had received the blow from the soldier's rifle, that left her severely afflicted. Mary experienced a death of lingering agony, and was buried in the family cemetery at Woodlands. The original gold watch is still in the possession of a Barnsley descendent in South America. Many years later, Mary's colorful story would also be related in the book *"In and Out of the Lines"* by Francis Howard, published in 1905, and republished in 1998, by the Etowah Valley Historical Society.)

Mary Quinn

During the summer of 1864, Barnsley compiled a carefully itemized list of his losses due to the Union invasion. The list consisted of eight pages. Although his home and gardens at Woodlands were spared from the torch, his total losses from the war still amounted to over $155,000. Since he had remained a British subject, he felt compelled to send a copy of the list to the British Consulate in Washington asking for reimbursement for his losses. Several years later he received notice that his plea was being considered. But the Barnsley's would never receive any compensation from the United States government.

List of Articles taken and destroyed, at Woodlands, Cass Co. Georgia, the residence of Godfrey Barnsley, by United States soldiers in May and June, 1864

2 Statues of Shepherds $30
2 Window Cornices, covered with velvet - carved and gilt ends. $30
1 Sett patent roller blinds
1 Large field telescope
1 pocket   do
Bronze hall lamp - $10.
Looking glass - $6.
    do   of dressing bureau
2 Large leather travelling bags
Box of Mathematical instruments, new - $35
Small do - $5.
Flute Nicholson's 8 keyed, silver mounted - $50.
Sett large, ivory bagatille balls + mace
2 Sword shaped ivory paper knives $6.
2 Engraved wafer stamps & glass wafer dish - $5.00
Aneroid barometer - $15.
Self registering thermometer
Microscope in case. $10
2 Magnifying glass - $5.
French - pebble eye glasses $6.
Claude Lorraine reflector $6.
2 Chinese tortoise shell sugar holders
2 Biscuit flower vases - 1 foot high
2 Large French china vases $35.
Silver & mother of pearl paper stand - $10.
Bohemian glass waiter, decanter, globlets & cups $50.
Bohemian glass water decanter & cup - $6.
Chrystal scent casket, in gilt stand $50.
Gilt metal flower vase, marble stand - $15.
Superior plated castors with embossed silver mouldings
2 Plated candlesticks with handles, embossed silver mouldings
6 Plated steel nut cracks - $12.
140 yds Brussels carpeting
2 rugs - $15 and $10. $25

2½ dozen dinner } ivory - handled,
2   "   dessert } bal......
Ivory handled carver & fork
6 Oyster Knives
Round of beef carver & fork - $4.
Patent corkscrew $4.
London patent trunk (cost £10. 10$) containing a large quantity of clothing & other articles - $200.
2 Hats - $10.
3 large common trunks destroyed - $18
Large, portable, rosewood, richly inlaid, writing desk, containing gold signet ring, gold pencil case, silver seal, a number of silver pencil cases, gold pens, & other small articles - $150.
1 Feather & 3 servants beds destroyed
Very large rich silk quilt - $300.
8 Marseilles counterpanes
18 large blankets, of which 6 very superior French
23 fine damask and 7 double damask napkins
15 table cloths - 3 large (double damask), 6 - three yds. square, 6 - three yards long & 2½ wide fine damask.
9 Linen sheets 1½/4
14 Cotton do 1½/4
2 linen bolster cases
8   do   pillow   do
4 superior bathing towels - $6.
1 Black silk dress $25.
New English straw bonnet - $12.
Bonner's Map of Georgia, on roller - $10.
Album containing drawings in colors, fine pencil, fine engravings &c &c.
French Illustrations of Byron, superbly bound in vellum.

Throughout the remainder of the year, Barnsley's morale seemed to be at an all time low. He naturally felt downtrodden, and seemed to lose much of his self-esteem. He had ceased to earn any income, many of his possessions were gone, and his children were scattered so that he felt lonely and depressed. His loyal Irish housekeeper, Mary Quinn, and a few live-in servants were his main companions during those turbulent days of 1864. Several of his business associates in New York knew of his plight, and offered to extend him credit for any amount he needed, but he had preferred not to get indebted unless the war should come to an end.

It was also during those dark and lonely days, that Mrs. C.V. Berrien, visited occasionally and continued to spark his interest in spiritualistic pursuits, once again strengthening his belief that Julia was in his midst.

Godfrey's son, Dr. George Barnsley, had also become impressed with the idea. In writing to his father, he referred to their mutual interest in believing that the dead would return to the places they had so loved in life.

After returning to his medical post in Virginia, George was also deeply disturbed to hear of his father's difficulties at Woodlands. He wrote in his "Journal of Poems", dated June 16, 1864:

> *"The Yankees have for a month held possession of my beloved home, and what they have done God only knows...But Pa has remained at Woodlands. Oh Woodlands, my home! There is no spot on earth, nor ever can be, around which are clustered so many recollections of joy, of sunbeams glittering on the rippling waters, of crystal springs, of flowers and golden-voiced butterflies...Oh god! Are they all gone forever? Oh, Woodlands! Woodlands! God forbid that my lot ever be separated from thee."*

Although Barnsley had suffered severely from the Union invasion, he was still saddened to receive the news that General McPherson had been killed in the battle of Atlanta on July 22, 1864. McPherson had, after all, acted as a gentleman, who had at least offered protection for Barnsley's property. As far as Barnsley was concerned, the North had lost the best General in their army.

In November of 1864, due to a $500 draft Barnsley received from The Pickers Gill Company, in New York, Mary Quinn was able to lift his spirits a bit. Since Godfrey had formally been accustomed to the finer things of life, and had not received any new clothing during the war, Mary was able to catch a train to Nashville, Tennessee to purchase some new garments. She soon returned with suits, coats, hats and shoes for him for which she paid $375.50. He was naturally very pleased by the diligent assistance of his loyal housemaid.

By the end of the year, Barnsley was again pleased when he received word that he had a new and healthy granddaughter born in Savannah. During General Sherman's invasion of North Georgia, Captain Baltzelle had cleverly slipped his wife, Julia, and her nephew, little Forrest Reid, through enemy lines and took them to Savannah. It was there, Julia had given birth to the child that she named for her deceased sister, Adelaide, and the child would be called "Addie." Little Addie came into the world on December 14, 1864, while General Sherman's advancing horde of "Blue Bellies" marched across Georgia to the sea.

Seven days later, on the 21st of December, Sherman captured the bustling Port City of Savannah, and all of its cotton. The city itself was spared from the torch, although its citizens suffered many afflictions from the Union forces. Julia soon wrote to her father:

"I despise these dratted Yankees more than ever.
The Captain delivered us from Woodlands to

escape Sherman's wrath, and now the old rascal is here. As soon as we are able to travel, little Forrest, the baby and myself, will be coming home to Woodlands."

Julia and her new baby daughter, along with little Forrest Reid arrived home in January of 1865. Barnsley was uplifted and happy to once again have some of his children with him at Woodlands.

After the capture of Savannah that claimed some $28,000,000, of its resources, the war moved on north to Virginia until finally forcing the surrender of Richmond on April 9, 1865, thus bringing to an end the bloody conflict between North and South. The long devastating war was over.

Barnsley's losses had been tremendous and he was still holding more than one hundred thousand dollars in worthless Confederate bonds. But he was greatly relieved that it was finally over. Even though he knew that recouping his losses would be a tremendous task, especially for a man of almost sixty, he was still willing to try.

By the first of July, England proved to be hungry for American cotton, just as Barnsley had anticipated. He soon received a letter from Fielden Brothers and Company of Liverpool, to send all the cotton he could ship, at six pence per pound delivered. An enthused Barnsley quickly began making plans to reopen his office in New Orleans.

CHAPTER 9

THE AFTERMATH

During all the excitement and confusion at the end of the war in Virginia, George and Lucien Barnsley lost track of one another, and finally began trudging their separate ways homeward. Lucien later related that he had spent some three weeks walking and sometimes hitching short buggy rides through the mountains of Kentucky, Tennessee and Georgia until eventually reaching Woodlands. Neither he nor George had heard from home in almost a year and after seeing so many homes and farms between Chattanooga and Adairsville destroyed by the war, he had prepared himself for the worst as far as Woodlands was concerned. On finally arriving at the front road gates, into Woodlands, he paused, peeking through the thickness of the trees to discover that the great tower of the manor was still standing. A tired and weary Lucien, with heavy beard, and trudging on swollen feet, almost bare, leaped with joy as he ran through the long carriage drive leading to the great manor. On finally reaching the entrance to the formal gardens, he could see the faithful family servant, Uncle Moses carrying on his daily chores in the parterre, although Moses did not recognize the heavy bearded Lucien. But when he cried out to "Uncle Moses," the old servant threw down his tools and rushed from the gardens. With tears of joy, Lucien ran into the open arms of Uncle Moses. It had been four long years since he had left for the war, and it felt good to once again see the family and to stand on Woodlands land.

On the other hand, Dr. George Barnsley had remained some days longer in Virginia before being discharged from the Medical Hospital at Richmond. After learning that his brother, Lucien, had already departed for home, he boarded a train to Knoxville, Tennessee, taking along with him as many of his medical instruments as he was able to carry. From there, he caught a boat and traveled down the Tennessee River to Chattanooga. Since many of the railroad bridges in the area had been destroyed or heavily damaged by war, George spent the next three days and nights, walking cautiously through Federal Pickets and heavy rainstorms to make the last sixty miles to Woodlands. He would later write in his "war journal" dated June 29, 1865:

> "It is hard to describe one's feelings on such occasions — to my great joy I found Julia, Lucian, Papa, Forrest and Little Addie, along with the old homestead still in existence, although Julia and Papa had been actually living on bread and water for a month."

After a brief reunion with the family and a few days of recuperating at the homestead, both George and Lucien began working to sustain the family and servants, picking berries and herbs from the woods and catching rabbits for food. On one occasion, Lucien was able to do some bartering at Kingston, by swapping a few bottles of brandy he had found for twenty pounds of bacon and some coffee.

But George Barnsley, a physician, and his brother, Lucien, a pharmacist, were not accustomed to handling such rugged transactions, and began to feel inadequate in trying to support Woodlands. The Barnsley brothers were no doubt beginning to appreciate the real blessing of a wealthy father who had once provided so abundantly.

It was a month later when Captain Baltzelle finally returned from his post at Augusta, eager to be reunited with his wife, Julia, and to see for the first time, his infant daughter, "Little Addie." The Captain, displaying the extraordinary foresight of a well-seasoned soldier, had already anticipated the plight of Woodlands, with the loss of its food supplies, livestock and other resources. He had therefore brought along with him a fine team of mules pulling a large covered wagon filled with clothing, seeds, and other supplies for the farm workers. Trailing behind the wagon was an old milk cow he had found straying somewhere in the wilderness and captured it, so the children of Woodlands would at least have milk to drink.

It was the strong and positive minded Captain Baltzelle that proved to be the financial savior of Woodlands immediately after the war. According to letters and stories handed down from that era, the family and their servants remembered the Captain working endless hours to teach every man, woman and child on the estate, the art of survival. He taught the men servants how to hunt for wild game and directed his brother-in-laws, George and Lucien, in building fish traps on the Etowah River, so the families could once again have some meat on their tables.

(Author's note: During an interview in 1956, with Emma Pritchett, (1870-1960) she related her mother's memoirs of Captain Baltzelle:)

"My mama told me lots of times it was Miss Addie's papa, the Captain, that saved all the folks at Barnsley after the war. It was sure enough hard times; wasn't no food left and wasn't no money either. But the Captain took care of em...showed em how to get food and make it through those bad

times. He was a fine man...everybody on the place loved him dearly!"

George soon teamed up with the Captain in planting new cornfields, but could not seem to keep up with him. He later described Baltzelle to be "as full of energy as a high pressure steam engine."

The Captain then prodded George to put one of the old stills back in operation to make whiskey and brandy. He instructed the younger ones to scavenge for coins and other valuables that he was sure had been dropped by Union soldiers. Barnsley's grandson Forrest Reid soon gathered a number of coins, and turned them over to his Aunt Julia, who used them to purchase flour and salt at Adairsville.

It was Captain Baltzelle who also urged the Barnsleys to lift up their heads and count their blessings. After all, "Woodlands" was still relatively in tact and none of their family had been killed or injured in the war. The land was still abundant, and he would teach them how to live off the land.

Such a life, however, was not very inspiring to the Barnsley Brothers, and they soon decided to follow their own professions by setting up a practice of medicine at Woodlands. But, due to the severe economic crisis that had gripped the South after the war, very few were able to pay for their services, so that their practice became, for the most part, a business of bartering. On one occasion, George had received a bushel of corn and two boxes of apples for delivering a "fine and healthy baby boy." By the spring of 1866, he had decided to close his medical office to try and find a more efficient way to earn a living. After returning from another futile "business venture" at Augusta on April 23, 1866, George found his sister, Julia, working in the fields with the Captain, her hands callused and dirty, and her skin darkened from the sun.

(<u>Author's note</u>: According to a story handed down by Julia's daughter, Addie Baltzell, George was very disturbed over the matter:

"I just cannot accept this terrible change in you!
It is totally uncivil and must be stopped at once!"
he scowled. But, Julia was quick to refute him -
"The entire South has changed, my dear brother
and we must change with it, if we expect to
survive!")

It seemed however, that George and Lucien Barnsley were not ready to accept such changes, nor at all satisfied with living under the new carpetbag government. Because of their dissatisfaction with the postwar South and their unwillingness to accept the oath of allegiance to the United States Government, the Barnsley Brothers soon became interested in a colonizing expedition to South America

THE SOUTHERN EXILE

Shortly after the war, the loss of the Confederacy and the extreme degradation of the South as a whole, left an emptiness in defeat that was devastating to most Southerners.

An old friend had written to Godfrey Barnsley from Savannah:

"We are surrounded by gloom, not even hope to
sustain us. My heart is so filled with an intensity
of hatred toward the authors of our misery, that I

cannot mollify. There is no happiness within or without. I cannot reconcile myself to this wretched servitude."

In reaction to their losses, many Southerners became eager to search for homes in other lands far from their familiar surroundings, where they would be free from Yankee domination. Some of them followed trails into the old west to track buffalo across the plains of Texas, or to pursue the gold fields of California. Others had felt they should completely break away from the reunited union to start a new life in Mexico, Central America, and even Europe. A great number of them, however, soon made the decision to sail for Brazil where the land was cheap, slavery was still legal, and there were numerous stories that the country had large deposits of gold just waiting to be discovered. Actually, immigrants had been warmly accepted in Brazil since 1860, when the government had written legislation that formalized the nation's invitation to free and self-governing colonies of immigrants. The Brazilian law makers had realized that colonies of immigrants would possibly provide additional medical assistance, build new roads, harness rivers, and increase agricultural production. In fact, the defeat of the U.S. Confederacy caused Brazilians to support even stronger policies that would import "new blood" into their country.

At the end of the war between the states, it was the Emperor of Brazil, Dom Pedro II, who officially encouraged former "Rebels" to consider Brazil as their new home. He had welcomed all new comers, and especially those skilled as doctors, engineers and builders, that he felt would be a great asset to his country. The immigrants were given a number of special benefits and land was offered to them at the low price of twenty-two and one half cents per acre. The confederates in turn expressed much interest in the hospitable country that offered them such advantages. Within a few years, more than one hundred

Southern families led by several different expeditions expatriated themselves to Brazil. In the years to follow, there would be an even greater number. It was to one such expedition led by J.J. "McMullen" of Texas, that the Barnsley Brothers followed. They soon left Bartow County, Georgia and arrived at Sao Paulo, Brazil in May of 1867. It was there they first settled down and became actively involved in establishing a new colony for the Confederados in Brazil.

(Author's note: The colony, known as "Vila Americana" has remained until the present day. Dr. George Barnsley did prove to be successful with his practice of medicine in Brazil, being for a time, the only skilled surgeon among 28,000 people. He would later meet and marry a southern immigrant from Mississippi, "Mary Laniera Emerson", who would bear him five children. Lucien would later marry in 1871 to Hannah Grady, also from Mississippi, who would bear him three children. More than one hundred and fifty of the Barnsley descendants live in Brazil today. In recent years five have returned to the United States. A book on the Brazilian immigration was released in the United States in 1987, by William Griggs entitled: *"The Elusive Eden"*)

In the fall of 1866, Godfrey Barnsley returned to New Orleans and reopened his business office that had been closed since 1862. Although he felt certain that cotton factoring in the South would never again be the same, he had hoped to recoup at least a portion of his business. Throughout the first half of 1867 he was encouraged by being able to fill several orders to European markets. But, the cost of doing business in New Orleans after the war, due to new restrictions and higher taxes imposed by the Federal Government, left him barely able to pay expenses. But, at least for the time being, he intended to keep trying.

Meanwhile, back on the homefront at Woodlands, Julia and the Captain were fighting their own battles with reconstruction. The robust Captain had taken over complete management of the Estate, and by working endless hours he and Julia, and the servants were able to at least earn an existence! In 1866, with the help of the servants, he raised a large field of cotton that produced five bales, weighing 416 pounds each. Since cotton was in high demand at the time, it brought an escalated price of twenty-eight cents per pound that returned them $583.00. The land also had an abundance of prime timber, and Baltzelle soon started his own lumber business with Mr. C.H. Hall at Hall's Mill near Woodlands. Although prices were very low, he was able to gain a little profit by furnishing lumber to the local towns, and also the city of Atlanta that was rebuilding after the war. In the year of 1867, he was able to negotiate a contract with the W & A Railroad to furnish specialized timber for the rebuilding of railroad bridges along the twelve miles of track between Adairsville and Kingston. It was the diligent effort of Captain Baltzelle that proved to be the driving force in rebuilding Woodlands, and much of the surrounding area after the war. He had grown to love and cherish his life in the country with Julia and his little daughter, Addie. It seemed that everyone at Woodlands had also grown to love and respect the jolly Captain, who had delivered them from the hells of war. Nevertheless, the days proved to be hard and lonely, so that Julia was forced to give up her social life, and stayed close to the homestead working with the Captain and her servants. She did, however, enjoy some social activity with her father's friend, the famous novelist, August Evans Wilson, from Mobile, who visited the Estate several times during the 1860's.

By that time, however, it had become evident that the strong perseverance and hard work of Captain Baltzelle was beginning to reap its rewards. But once again, Woodlands would be struck by tragedy.

On the cold frosty morning of February 14, 1868, the Captain and his workers were rebuilding a war damaged railroad bridge near Hall's Mill, when a large timber fell out of control. Baltzelle quickly intervened to protect his men, only to be struck by the timber, and his body thrown down a long embankment. The strong and jolly Captain, who had came through the war without a scratch, was killed almost instantly. According to a worker, John C. Kerr, the Captain's concern for Julia and his "Little Addie" were the last words he uttered. His crushed remains were returned to a weary, heartbroken Julia, by Rev. C.W. Howard, and buried in the family cemetery south of the Manor. Everyone at Woodlands was deeply grieved by the sudden death of Captain Baltzelle.

(Author's note: A marker still stands inside the little graveyard at Barnsley Gardens, "In Remembrance of the Man who Saved Woodlands after the War, Captain James Peter Baltzelle.")

Down in New Orleans on February 15, Godfrey Barnsley received a telegram:

"Captain B. is dead. Come. J.B.B."

Godfrey left on the early morning train and arrived at Woodlands three days later where he would spend some time with his daughter, Julia, and his four year old granddaughter, Addie. Little Addie was too young to fully understand the loss of her father, but in the days to come, her mother, Julia, suffered tremendously from the emotional shock of the Captain's death. But, when Barnsley returned to New Orleans in the fall, Julia felt responsible for everyone at Woodlands and decided, rather suddenly, to buckle down to the tremendous work at hand. She was not in the least willing to give up what her beloved Captain had worked so hard to achieve, even though she knew that such an undertaking would be a mammoth task without his strength and guidance.

In the months that followed, Julia would become well seasoned to the hardships of reconstruction at Woodlands. Many of her days were spent gleaning the fields with her servants, digging for turnips and roots or anything else she could find to keep her household from starving until more crops could be planted and harvested.

However, survival alone was not the only problem facing Julia. She would experience many more hardships and disappointments while struggling to save Woodlands.

Julia was especially saddened when her sister's husband, John K. Reid, a traveling sea merchant of Londonderry, Ireland, arrived at Woodlands to reclaim his ten year old son, Godfrey Forrest Reid. Julia was naturally very attached to the child, and felt he was still too young to be taken away from her. But, Reid had hoped his son would follow in his footsteps, and was determined to take the boy out to sea. A grieving Julia soon bid her last good-bye to young Godfrey Forrest Reid, the child she had lovingly reared and cherished since his birth.

(Author's note: Godfrey Forrest Reid grew up to spend his life as a missionary in South Africa. Although he would correspond with his family at Woodlands through the years, and also became a legal heir to the family estate, Julia would never see him again.)

As the harsh days of reconstruction continued, Julia was also plagued by land squatters and night thieves hiding out on her lands. Some were small farmers who had lost their homesteads to General Sherman's torches, while others, for the most part, were stragglers or freed slaves who had no place to go after the war. But, Julia did not have the heart to turn away those of extreme need, and did her utmost to handle them in a civilized manner. Since she fully believed that education would be the only key to survival under the New Government, she spent many of her winter days holding classes to teach her younger Negro servants and the Irish farm children to read and write.

(<u>Author's note:</u> Julia's Negro servant, "Ned Phinizy" (1842-1937) was issued a "Certificate of Merit" for his extraordinary learning abilities, and another one for his outstanding horticultural achievements in the Woodlands Gardens. Ned proved to be loyal to the Barnsleys throughout his life and became a well respected citizen of the area. He later became the first honorary black member of a white church near Woodlands. Ned was also a musician and was a builder of musical instruments. - (Notes taken from the family records of Rose Phinizy of Freedom, Pennsylvania:)

Uncle Ned Phinizy

Julia's methods of teaching, however, did not go unnoticed by some of the local segregationists that had disagreed with her style of handling Negro slaves and Irish immigrants. According to the accounts of several of the older residents, Julia finally experienced a threatening demonstration of terror staged by the Klu Klux Klan near the main gates into Woodlands.)

As the old timers later remembered, it was such hard life experiences that turned the genteel Julia into an iron willed mistress, toting a shotgun to protect her precious Woodlands.

During those turbulent days after the Captain's death, Julia's sister, Anna Gilmour, had advised her to get away from Woodlands and come to England where she and Little Addie could enjoy a life of ease and comfort. Although such a move would have easily delivered Julia from her many hardships, she refused. It was completely against her nature to abandon the homestead, and she still felt responsible for every man, woman, and child at Woodlands. Also, since the South was beginning to rebuild from the war, Julia was convinced that the value of lumber and cotton would go very high, and Woodlands would eventually rise again. With all the hunger and suffering she had been forced to bare, Julia was still determined to remain, keeping her faith in the grace of God that one day life would be better... *"We must count our blessings and keep our faith that we will overcome, and Woodlands will never again go hungry."*

Julia and her servants struggled to continue operating the Captain's lumber business, although it provided only a meager income. In the spring of the following year, Julia joined forces with "Robert Reed," a young half Cherokee farmer, who became her overseer and established a new method of share farming that would relieve some of her burdens. "Reed" became a close friend and ally, who protected the young widow, Julia, from her predators.

In the meantime, down in New Orleans, Godfrey Barnsley had found southern reconstruction under the New Government to be anything but a blessing. Although he was able to do some business, his expenses for 1868 were so heavy, he had not been able to provide any financial assistance for Julia and Little Addie back at Woodlands. He wrote to his daughter on May 18, 1869:

"Almost everything has changed now...and there is such a laxity of morals among the commercial class. I cannot accept it. Taxes are enormous, income taxes, city and United States, in this free country are now very much heavier than in England. Everything financially has gone against me. It was a great error in returning here, as I could have lived in the country on my own labor."

Barnsley's bitterness over the situation was also reflected in a letter to his sons, living in Brazil:

"Do not return to this country. You are in a much better one. Demoralization is very high in the United States, and the entire government, Federal, State and City, is a gigantic system of plunder. Honesty in trade is the exception, with bribery and corruption everywhere. I sincerely hope you are keeping clear of politics."

Barnsley left New Orleans on June 29, 1869, eager to spend the summer at his North Georgia Estate. But, after arriving there on July 2nd, he was immediately disturbed over the state of affairs at Woodlands, as he wrote to his daughter Anna in England:

"There is so much to do at Woodlands, and nothing to do it with! — I want to get away from here unless fortunate enough to make it a permanent resting place. This place is a mess, little crops and many weeds and I am considering letting it and myself go to the dogs. I am heartily tired of it and everything else!"

But, after relaxing for a few days in the peacefulness of Woodlands, and finding that Julia's new overseer looked promising, some of his depression seemed to subside. He then made plans to do some repairs and reroofing of his manor house and kitchen wing.

In earlier years, Barnsley would have hired laborers to handle such a project, but now he felt they were too expensive. He was determined that he and one of the servants alone could handle the chore. Although he was now sixty-four years old, and not accustomed to such manual tasks, he worked each day from dawn till dark, throughout the hot summer until the roofs were covered anew. Barnsley still felt responsible to keep the estate in repair for Julia and Little Addie, his only family left at Woodlands.

While spending the summer there, he was delighted to hear from his sons, George and Lucien, in Brazil, and to learn that they had married well. George had written that his wife, Mary Laniera Emerson, was not of a wealthy family, but felt that he was "the most fortunate man in Brazil" to be getting her. Godfrey was also pleased to hear that he was progressing well as a physician earning over $5,000 in gold in 1869, and that the money would go twice as far there as in the United States.

George and Mary Laniera Emerson Barnsley
(Courtesy of George Barnsley Family)

Barnsley at least felt somewhat better about the future of his children, when he returned to New Orleans in late 1869. But, shortly after his return, he found business to be so depressed that he expected to have to give up. He wrote:

> *"Everything goes against us. I hoped there would have been a change in the current of my ill luck, but it continues, due to the restrictions imposed on the south by the northern radicals and the new Trans Atlantic telegraph cable that has rendered cotton, strictly a business of gambling and I will take no part in it."*

Barnsley could no longer seem to cope with the situation. He was also concerned over how to keep Woodlands operating with the rising cost of farming and other maintenance. He had once thought of trying to sell the place, but knew he would be forced to take a great loss, since the value of Georgia farm property had fallen so low after the war. Since his younger business partner, the "Baron" Charles H. Von Schwartz was also experienced in the business of farm real estate and other matters pertaining to the New Federal laws, Barnsley decided to send him up to Woodlands to evaluate his situation there. Also considering that Julia had been living a life of loneliness since the Captain's death, he had arranged for the Baron to escort his friend, a Miss Jensen from Germany to spend some time at Woodlands with Julia, who could in turn teach her the English language. Barnsley had felt their visit would be a means of solace for Julia.

It was while the "Baron" Von Schwartz was visiting Woodlands in the fall of 1869, that he became romantically attracted to the young widow, Julia Baltzelle. Before departing for New Orleans in January of 1870, the Baron proposed marriage to Julia and offered her a lavish home in New Orleans. But, Julia's heart and soul was still tied up in maintaining Woodlands and now she seemed more contented operating the estate with her overseer, Robert Reed. Julia had not been romantically attracted to the Baron and it was also a bit soon after the Captain's death to consider a new relationship. She therefore refused the Baron's proposal.

During the following year, Barnsley's business improved slightly, due to receiving consignments for the shipping of rail iron. But due to high duties imposed by the New Federal Government, he only earned $1,870.84, before deductions, leaving him a net profit of less than $1,000.00, for the year. It was no doubt depressing to a man who had ten years earlier, earned more than $100,000, in one year, but he was at least able to pay some expenses and send a few rations to his daughter, Julia. On March 17, 1871, he shipped by rail to Kingston a barrel of sugar, twenty gallons of kerosene, one bushel of malt, a box of soap, and two dresses for Little Addie. He had wanted to send more, but explained that he couldn't, as he wrote:

> *"In my old age I have to be content with obscurity and the extravagant sum of $75.00 per month for rent, board, fire, light and washing. I economize here in New Orleans so as to keep Woodlands from going to wreck."*

While suffering through the pressures of a failing business, Barnsley had also began to notice signs of declining health. He had begun to suffer from pains in the back, and developed a serious cough, so that his doctor encouraged him to get away from the extreme heat of New Orleans and the pressures of business. He decided to spend another summer at Woodlands to relax in the cooler mountain air. Barnsley had hoped on his arrival this time, to find Julia under better circumstances, but, much to his regret, he learned that her overseer had left unexpectedly, and she was again struggling to keep Woodlands operating. Godfrey wrote in his memoirs:

> *"Julia is farming. Chiefly on shares with both white and colored. But, nothing changes! She is losing money here, almost as fast as I am in New Orleans!"*

Barnsley spent a rather lonely summer at Woodlands with Julia and Little Addie, making no visits and receiving very few visitors. He remained nervous over business frustrations, and his health was growing steadily worse, so that he was under the impression he would not last very long. His son, George, wrote from Brazil that he believed it would be better for his father's health if he would remain at Woodlands, and never return to

New Orleans, and that he would be willing to help support him if he would do so. But, Barnsley wrote to him:

> *"Thank you for your offer of funds to enable me to remain here, but so long as my strength lasts, my nature requires me to work. But, I do look forward to the change of existence."*

Although Barnsley had been a member of the Anglican Church, he had never shown any strong religious enthusiasm. However, he did speak often of his belief in God, and constantly admonished his children to obey the Christian principles they had been taught. Also, he frequently engaged in theological debates and discussions with those of Atheism, to try and convince them of the existence of God, and of a future state. When writing to an old friend in 1870, he showed that he still maintained his original beliefs concerning mankind:

> *"I cannot see in the war in which so many lives are lost any reason to doubt the goodness of the Supreme Ruler. All human actions determine the results and if mankind will do wrong they bring on themselves the inevitable consequences of a violation of moral law."*

A tired and weary Godfrey Barnsley

The summer of 1871, was the last summer Godfrey spent at Woodlands. In the fall, he returned to his office on the third floor of the Canal Street Bank in New Orleans in hopes of generating new business for the upcoming year. But, again, he earned only enough to keep his expenses paid. After finally coming to the conclusion that he was too old to keep pace with the new methods of cotton factoring, he turned the control of his New Orleans operation over to Charles H. Von Schwartz, who had by now became an active partner in the business. Barnsley had placed a great deal of confidence in Von Schwartz, as he wrote:

> *"My dividing with him my interest in the business is a great help to me. I have known him intimately*

for many years and shared an office with him for two years. He is a man of great integrity, handling his business affairs well."

Von Schwartz soon opened a new office on the Mississippi River at St. Louis, to represent Barnsley and himself, in a new type of cotton commission business.

In the spring of 1872, Barnsley requested that the "Baron" take another trip to Woodlands, to again check on conditions with Julia and Little Addie at the homestead. On arriving, the Baron found that Julia was still fighting for survival and so unhappy living alone. Therefore, he once again asked for her hand in marriage to which this time, she readily accepted. After all, the Baron was truly a gentleman who, also, had the financial means to rebuild the war trodden estate. Once again Julia had placed her father's Woodlands above everything else in her life.

Charles Henry Von Schwartz and Julia Barnsley Baltzelle were married at "Woodlands" on July 8, 1872. The next day they left on their wedding trip to Lookout Mountain, Tennessee, taking Little Addie along with them. The Baron spent a total of $95.65, on the trip for train tickets, hotels and entertainment.

The Baron Von Schwartz

Julia Barnsley Baltzelle
Von Schwartz

Little Addie

Meanwhile, down in New Orleans, Godfrey Barnsley's health had continued to fail, until his doctor had finally diagnosed his condition as tuberculosis. It would have no doubt been better for his health to return to Woodlands, but Godfrey had already made up his mind that he would remain at his office in New Orleans until the end of his days.

The Baron Von Schwartz soon made plans to take Julia and little "Addie" to his elegant home in New Orleans, where Julia could be close to her father, and also have some time away from the burden of operating Woodlands. But, since Julia was still deeply concerned over matters at the homestead, the Baron began searching for a reliable overseer to take charge of the estate.

A few weeks later, Von Schwartz hired Jake Sherman, a

young industrious farmer, who had come highly recommended, to be the overseer of Woodlands. Jake was a very intelligent, hard working man, who had both the will and ingenuity to make Woodlands prosper. He readily cleansed the estate of its undesirables, and employed new share farmers, so that the lands again became productive. Jake Sherman and his descendants would prove to be a blessing for the Barnsley Estate for generations to come.

(Author's note: Jake Sherman married Catherine Ward of Halls Mill and reared a large family at Woodlands. His son, George Sherman, born there in 1878, would take his father's place as the Woodlands' overseer, at the turn of the Twentieth Century. George would later marry Allie Hutcherson, and rear twelve children at Woodlands. Many of the Sherman descendants have remained near Woodlands.)

Jake Sherman (1841-1933)

George Sherman (1878-1968)

(Courtesy of Ralph Sherman & Francis Blalock)

Julia Barnsley Von Schwartz remained in New Orleans, caring for her father until the end. Death came to Godfrey Barnsley on June 7, 1873. His body was embalmed, placed in a coffin of copper and shipped to Woodlands by way of the railroad.

Three days later, the Baron, Julia and Little Addie accompanied Barnsley's body on the train to the little depot at Halls Mill near Woodlands. According to Barnsley's granddaughter, every man, woman and child on the estate followed close behind, singing their hymns as the coffin passed through the front gates into Woodlands. The old Merchant Prince was laid to rest in the little family graveyard alongside his infant son, Godfrey Junior, his daughter, Adelaide, and his son-in-law, Captain Baltzelle. Barnsley had requested that no marker be placed on his grave since he felt it would be of no real benefit and preferred that such funds be spent on those still living at Woodlands. The news of his death brought much sadness to his friends and family around the world and especially throughout the South who remembered him, not only as an international trade figure, but also for the important role he had played in developing the Cherokee wilderness of Northwest Georgia. Godfrey Barnsley would also be remembered as a well disciplined man of strong principle, who believed that, "right was right, but wrong was wrong, and a man's word should be his golden bond."

Godfrey Barnsley left to his children all of his property, real and personal or mixed, but it was never admitted to probate.

Since the estate had progressed so well under the leadership of Jake Sherman, the new Mrs. Julia Von Schwartz and her nine-year-old daughter, Addie, soon followed the Baron to his new business in St. Louis where they would reside for the next three years.

In 1877, the Von Schwartz family returned to Woodlands to make it a permanent home, at which time the Baron sold off a few of the unproductive land lots, and began refurbishing the entire estate. He hired three full-time gardeners to beautify and keep the grounds, and supported Jake Sherman in expanding the farm and timber operations so that the estate would again, become a self-supporting enterprise.

While Von Schwartz strove to rebuild Woodlands, he also provided well for Julia, and his stepdaughter, Addie, that he had fully accepted as his own daughter. As Addie grew into a young woman, the Baron seemed to cater to her every whim, furnishing her parties and expensive clothing, along with her own collection of fine thoroughbred horses.

The older residents of Woodlands later remembered that Addie Baltzelle could sport a different horse for each day of the week.

Although it would be a long time before the South would fully recover from the depredations of war, it became apparent that Von Schwartz was gradually returning Woodlands to its former splendor.

However, the successful ventures of the Baron would prove to be short lived. After returning from a business trip to South America, Charles Henry Von Schwartz contracted a rare illness and died in New Orleans on January 31, 1885. Addie Baltzelle was naturally crushed over the untimely death of her stepfather and the only father she had been able to remember. Julia had the Baron's body brought home to Woodlands and buried in the family cemetery alongside her father, and her first husband, so that the little graveyard had finally become quite cosmopolitan. Three men from foreign worlds were now all resting together on the same little knoll. The Englishman, Godfrey Barnsley, along with Captain Baltzelle of French Huguenot descent and now, the Baron Von Schwartz of German nobility.

After the Baron's death, the future of the family estate, once again, became the responsibility of the strong-willed women of Woodlands, Julia Von Schwartz and her daughter, Addie Baltzelle.

A war-trodden Julia

Addie Baltzelle
(Courtesy of Lollie Murphy)

THE RETURN OF DR. BARNSLEY

By the mid 1880's, due to a series of financial upsets in Brazil, Dr. George Barnsley felt that living there was no longer an advantage and wrote to his sister, Julia, requesting that she send him funds to return to Woodlands. Also, through the years, Dr. Barnsley had become deeply interested in prospecting for gold and rare minerals in Brazil, and now believed that his father's north Georgia estate was probably rich in such minerals and possibly even gold.

It was in 1888, that George began transporting his family to the United States. After arriving at the old homestead, George began to assist Julia in maintaining the houses and grounds, and also began prospecting for gold and minerals on the land. But, only a short time later, George seemed to have second thoughts concerning "Woodlands" and began conducting a survey of his father's estate, and all of its furnishings in order to advertise a sale of the place. His plan was to have the proceeds from such, divided equally among the family. But, Dr. Barnsley's decision was quickly challenged by his sister, Julia Von Schwartz, who was not at all pleased with his new plan. Julia was quick to remind her brother that he had deserted Woodlands after the war to chase his dreams into South America, while she had remained on the estate, suffering through all the hardships, and the loss of two husbands, to preserve her father's Woodlands.

Julia had unselfishly devoted her life to the homestead, and was not in the least interested in selling off any more of the Woodlands land, except for a few small tracts that she donated for religious or humanitarian purposes. During that year, she had donated two acres of land for a church to be built on the Obediah Snow land tract, about two miles north of the Manor. The Snow Springs Baptist Church was established at that time. The original building would be replaced by a new one in 1916, that would remain until modern times. She had also provided land for the Barnsley School that she and the Baron Von Schwartz had established to educate the children of Woodlands. The school, erected beside the Barnsley Church about a mile from the Manor, would remain in use until the late 1930's.

Dr. George Barnsley was later, of course, granted a portion of land in which to provide his family a home and a place to practice his profession. He also continued to prospect the lands for gold and minerals. George later claimed his portion of the family heirlooms, and opened a practice of medicine at Woodlands that he would operate until 1895.

CHAPTER 10

A NEW ERA

On a lazy September afternoon in 1889, the southbound train from Chattanooga made its daily stop at the small railroad junction of Halls Mill, Georgia. The steaming locomotive had no sooner chugged to a halt, when a tall dark stranger stepped down from the train, quickly scanned his surroundings, and sauntered off into the General Store alongside the railroad.

The strikingly handsome stranger, with his olive skin, deep brown eyes and full handlebar moustache soon caught the attention of everyone in the store. But, the man was careful not to reveal his true profession as he began to inquire about the local area. After learning from the storekeeper that two single women were in charge of the great Barnsley Estate, barely three miles distant, he gathered up his baggage and checked into a local boarding house, under the name of B.F. Armington. On the next morning, Armington started off on the dusty three-mile journey to Woodlands.

On that afternoon, the overseer, Jake Sherman and his son, George, watched from their front porch as the man came trudging down the road toward the rear entrance gates into Woodlands. Jake kept a watchful eye on the stranger as he crossed through the village compound and up the hillside, until finally reaching the front steps of the overseer's house.

(<u>Author's note:</u> From an interview conducted with George Sherman in 1956, came the following:

"He told my Pa his name was B.F. Armington from up in Pennsylvania, and, of course, we could tell he was a Yankee, by the way he talked. He wanted to know if Pa could use an extra hand on the place; said he could do just about anything, and was willing to work cheap. But, right away, Pa got suspicious of the fellow. He just couldn't figure out why a Yankee would come all the way down to Georgia looking for work, since the North had lots more money than the south in those days. But, Mr. Armington said the weather here was better for his health. Well, as it worked out, Pa decided to give the man a chance at saw milling and farm labor and Mr. Armington went to work the next day...and you know, the fellow turned out to be a pretty good worker...Pa liked him, and so did everybody else. But ya know, he still felt like the man was keeping some kind of secret up his sleeve. Because, after he got to know Armington better, he could tell he was really a smart man, and had too much education to be working at hard labor, for just twenty-five cents a day and his grub. But, of course, Pa figured time would tell, and sure enough it did!"

As the weeks passed, B.F. Armington performed his daily duties well, while spending his evenings and weekends secretly scouting out the Barnsley's lands. Some of the servants had noticed the new worker seemed to have a strange hobby of collecting small fossils from the fields and forests of Woodlands.

From a story handed down through the family, it was one afternoon while George Barnsley was down on the creek panning for gold, he suddenly caught sight of B.F. Armington, gathering soil samples from a distant field. George quickly set out to investigate the intruder and the two men soon came face to face. After a rather harsh confrontation, B.F. Armington was forced to reveal his true profession. The mysterious farm worker at Woodlands had turned out to be a professional chemist and mineralogist from Pottstown, Pennsylvania.

B.F. Armington, chemist

For several years "Armington" had been experimenting with formulas to develop certain products made from pine pulp and cotton fibers. He had therefore decided to come south where such raw materials were plentiful. He had also worked in the laboratories of the noted American chemist and inventor,

Charles Hall, who had developed a practical process of mining and producing aluminum from bauxite ore. After researching a number of geological surveys, Armington was convinced that the Appalachian foothills of Northwest Georgia contained rich deposits of bauxite. He had therefore been looking for large bodies of land in the area in which to secretly explore his theories. The chemist had also been experimenting with a number of new inventions he had created.

(Author's note: In a letter to a manufacturing firm, "Armington" had already predicted the 1900's to be, "the century of inventions that would change the entire world.")

When Armington finally explained to George Barnsley that his findings at Woodlands could possibly make the family wealthy, the Doctor was immediately intrigued. George quickly decided the chemist would be a great asset to his own aspirations of mining and soon offered to join with him in prospecting the land.

After working a few days with Armington, George confronted his sister, Julia, explaining that the new worker was actually a very brilliant mineralogist who would prove to be an asset to Woodlands. He suggested they should provide him quarters at Woodlands, possibly in the guest cottage. But, Julia was naturally confused over the ordeal, since Armington had only been hired as a laborer, and was against her brother's idea. Neither did she have any desire to become involved in her brother's mining "dreams" that she considered a waste of time, and urged him to return to his medical profession to earn a living. A short time later, however, when Julia and her daughter, Addie, were introduced to the charming chemist, things began to change. B.F. Armington soon took up residence in Godfrey Barnsley's cottage.

It was then, George Barnsley agreed to work with the chemist to establish a mining operation at Woodlands of which Armington would have full control. Although George Barnsley believed he had already discovered bauxite ore on the place, it was in the year of 1891, that the first bauxite mines were excavated on the Barnsley property. B.F. Armington cleverly named them the "Julia Mines," that was naturally quite-gratifying to the Mistress of Woodlands, Julia Barnsley Von Schwartz. The new company was registered in the State of Georgia as follows:

CABLE ADDRESS,
WILLIS, CHARLESTON, S. C.

USE SCOTT'S CODE, 1890,
or
WATKINS' CODE, 1881.

Armington & Company,

MINERS AND EXPORTERS

OF HIGH GRADE

Bauxite.

Armington & Company

During the early 1890's the mining venture proved to be a profitable enterprise, with B.F. Armington as president and Dr. George Barnsley serving as a clerk and chief assistant. The operation would soon be expanded into other areas, so that the business of mining "bauxite" would eventually become a thriving industry throughout all of Northwest Georgia.

As Armington's mining company was once again turning Woodlands into a self-supporting estate, the chemist seemed to also be gaining more clout with Julia Von Schwartz and her daughter, Addie. When Armington felt he had won their full confidence, he requested Julia to build him a laboratory at Woodlands, in which to develop his own formulas. Armington, in turn, promised to make her rich. Since his mining venture was proving successful, it was easy for Julia to answer in the affirmative. A large portion of Godfrey Barnsley's cottage was soon renovated into a modern laboratory for the day and age. From that time on, it was apparent that both Julia and her daughter, Addie, fully supported the chemist in experimenting with his new formulas at Woodlands.

But, as the days passed, George Barnsley began to realize that the opportunist, B.F. Armington, was gaining much control over his sister, Julia, and the family estate. He could also see the "charming" chemist was developing a strong social relationship with both the ladies, and especially his niece, Addie Baltzelle, that he felt was a bit out of order. But after confronting the matter, George wrote that his feelings were either ignored or "hooted" at by his sister, Julia. George seemed to lose much of his zeal in working at Woodlands after finding that his sister, Anna Gilmour of London, and his nephew, Godfrey Forrest Reid of South Africa, had transferred all their rights to the homestead back to Julia Von Schwartz; which gave her the majority of control.

Shortly thereafter when Dr. Barnsley received word that medical surgeons were again urgently needed in Brazil, and also fully believing that he could still locate the notorious "Lost Sea" of gold in Brazil's land of the Sertao, he immediately made plans to return to South America.

It was in the summer of 1895, that George transported a boxcar load of his father's heirlooms to be sold in New York, and went from there on to Brazil. The burden of handling his final business on the estate was left to his wife, Mary Laniera Emerson Barnsley, who remained at Woodlands with her children until 1898, at which time they returned to Brazil. Mary Laniera would also prove to be one of the strong willed women of Woodlands.

(Author's note: George Barnsley would remain in Brazil until his death in 1918. Many of his descendants would also remain near the colony of Vila Americana. Lucien

Barnsley had also remained in Brazil until his death in 1892, and most of his descendants still reside in South America.)

Dr. Barnsley later wrote in his "Memoirs of Woodlands", that his decision to return to Brazil in 1895, was also encouraged by B.F. Armington, who had suggested that South America was filled with bauxite ore, and that he should explore the possibilities of forming a new company there. But, George stated that the entire maneuver was only a manipulation of B.F. Armington and Julia Von Schwartz to get him away from Woodlands.

By the summer of 1897, it had become evident that Addie Baltzelle was romantically involved with B.F. Armington who was ten years her senior. They were soon engaged, and a wedding was planned at Woodlands, but not before B.F. Armington would reveal his most well kept secret. According to the older residents of Woodlands, it was after returning from a month long trip to Pennsylvania that Armington suddenly confronted Addie and revealed his true identity. He soon confessed that his legal name was B.F.A. Saylor, who also had a wife and two children back in Pennsylvania. But, now he was divorced and freed from a long tumultuous marriage and was still determined to marry Addie Baltzelle.

But, both Addie and her mother were deeply shocked and felt betrayed. Older servants remembered that the incident caused quite a stir at the great manor, and the wedding was postponed. Some days later, however, when the disturbance had settled a bit, Addie agreed to carry on with the wedding under one condition. Since Saylor was rightfully responsible for his children, Addie felt the only correct principle to follow was to demand that he bring them South and make them a home at Woodlands, where he could care for them properly. The extraordinary integrity and loyal principles of Godfrey Barnsley had now seemed to surface in his granddaughter, Addie Baltzelle.

In time to come, Saylor's teenaged children, "Ross" and "Blanche" Saylor were brought to Woodlands where they would remain for many years.

Benjamin Franklin Armington Saylor and Adelaide Baltzelle were married at Woodlands on December 21, 1897, and moved into the Barnsley mansion with Julia Von Schwartz.

B.F.A. Saylor

Addie Baltzelle Saylor

Shortly after the wedding, Saylor again indulged himself into his work in the laboratories. It was there he developed a new process of making a refined paper from wood pulp that also proved successful. He therefore established another new company at Woodlands, and joined forces with a local attorney to secure stock investors for the firm. Eventually a large number of shares would be sold with Saylor holding control of the capital stock in the company known as: The Standard Turpentine and Wood Pulp Company of Georgia.

A Certificate of Stock
from
The Standard Turpentine and Wood Pulp Company

A large number of company shares were eventually sold to stock holders across the nation. B.F.A. Saylor opened offices for his new company at Woodlands, and in Kingston, and Rome, Georgia.

see next page →

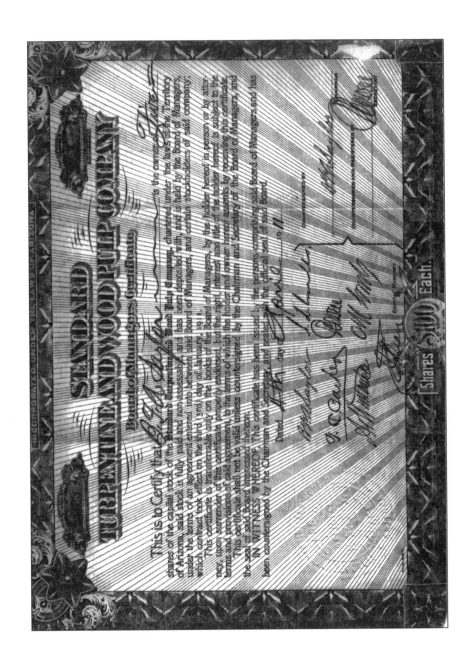

170

Saylor also labored tirelessly to perfect a formula to produce an "acetate silk" product, made from the fibers of cotton and pine wood pulp that would later become known as "rayon."

In the years to come, the chemist would also gain interest in several other companies of the South. In 1899, he was appointed vice president and general manager of the Gulf States Portland Cement Company, and in 1902, he was listed as a vice president of the Rome Iron Works in Floyd County, Georgia. He also developed a watering device for poultry growers and became an active member of the F.S.A. Agricultural Engineers of London, England.

In 1899, Julia Barnsley Von Schwartz contracted a mental disorder and died just before the turn of the twentieth century, leaving B.F.A. Saylor and her daughter, "Addie," to maintain Woodlands. Julia was laid to rest in the little family graveyard, among the three men she had so loved in life – Captain Baltzelle, the Baron Von Schwartz, and her father, Godfrey Barnsley, thus ending another generation of Barnsleys at Woodlands.

CHAPTER 11

A NEW GENERATION

By the turn of the twentieth century, the great Woodlands Estate had ultimately passed into the hands of B.F.A. Saylor and his wife, Addie. By that time the place had become known as Barnsley Gardens and the remaining three thousand acres of land, some called the Saylor Place.

Four beautiful children, Mary, Preston, Harry and Julia, were born to the Saylors at Barnsley Manor. The eldest child, Mary, born in 1898, died during infancy. Although Saylor was truly devoted to his children, it seemed that he and his wife never became fully compatible. As Addie grew older, she also began to believe in the shadowy world of spiritualism, insisting that her spirit ancestors were constantly in her midst. She often claimed to see her grandmother, Julia Barnsley, strolling through the gardens, and would hear the Barnsley children of the past, playing in the Manor – or the sound of her grandfather sliding back his chair in his upstairs office. But, Saylor never became comfortable with Addie's mystical passages, nor could he see the sense of such maneuvers. It seemed, therefore, he preferred to spend much of his leisure time in the company of others.

By the early 1900's, some had begun to look upon the charming chemist as a legendary "playboy."

(Author's note: From an interview in 1960 with an elder resident of Barnsley Gardens, Louella Johnson, (1890-1974.).

> *"Mr. Saylor often staged large business parties with his friends, flowing with wine, song, and beautiful women, which naturally affected his relationship with Addie. And sometimes he would go off on drinking "flights" with others, spending days at a time away from Miss Addie."*

The majority, however, still remembered Saylor as a well-respected chemist, and a man good for his word, who had contributed greatly to the economic development of Northwest Georgia.

(Author's note: Simon Crowder, who had worked as a young man for Saylor, stated in an interview in 1955.)

> *"He was a very colorful fellow, and one of the smartest men I ever met. He was good and fair to work for and always paid for everything he owed me!"*

After taking control of the Barnsley Estate, B.F.A. Saylor established new saw mills, and expanded the peach orchards that turned into a lucrative business. He also supported the overseer, George Sherman, in developing new and better methods of farming the lands.

George Sherman would later remember it being a bit ironic that "Saylor" had been hired as a laborer, and only ten years later, everyone on the estate was working for B.F. Armington Saylor. But, George also reminisced that his family fared quite well, while working under Saylor.

However, the cost of operating such a mammoth estate in the post war south proved to be astronomical. Saylor therefore, began to supplement the lean periods by selling or trading off some of the less productive lands, and by making whiskey and brandy in the old stills on the property.

It was also during Saylor's time that a series of misfortunate events took place at Barnsley Gardens. First of all, the chemist lost control of his acetate "rayon" formula that he was sure had been smuggled from his laboratory by a member of his own firm. The incident resulted in Saylor filing an $80,000 lawsuit against a manufacturer of the product, but would never receive any compensation from the venture.

Secondly, a strange, most horrid incident occurred on the property during those days. One afternoon while the Saylor children along with a family servant were strolling past the family cemetery, they suddenly detected one of the graves had been entered. On investigating, they were shocked to discover it was the original burial mound of the old merchant prince himself, Godfrey Barnsley. His skeletal remains had been partially removed from the coffin, and the right hand had been severed at the wrist and taken away. B.F.A. Saylor believed the perpetrator was a superstitious Negro worker, who lived on the place, but was never able to fully support the allegation. Various stories, ranging from an Indian curse to Yankee thievery began to circulate, and the High Sheriff was summoned to investigate the brutal act. But the real mystery behind the strange event was never solved.

STORY OF SKELETON HAND

B. F. A. Saylor, of Rome, Tells of
Desecration of Grave.

GRAND JURY IS INVESTIGATING

Parties Who Opened Grave of Godfrey Barnesley, Partially Exhumed
Body of Mrs. Schwartz.

Rome, Ga., January 30.—(Special.)—As
particulars of the desecration of Godfrey
Barnesley's grave come to light, the deed
assumes even a more grewsome aspect
than when first reported through The
Constitution's columns.

B. F. A. Saylor, president of the Rome
Petroleum and Iron Company, has lived
at the historic Barnesley home for many
years. About this home and the family
which gives it the name there clusters
ante-bellum stories as rare and stirring
as ever filled any work of fiction. Here
is the spot supposed to be the scene of
Mrs. Wilson's powerful romance, "St.
Elmo."

Mr. Saylor, in an interview today, detailed the story of the exhuming of
Godfrey Barnesley's body and the sever-
ing of the skeleton hand.

"The old family burying ground," said
he, "is about 300 yards south of the
house and is grown about with dense
wood and underbrush, which afforded
the vandal or vandals excellent conceal-
ment for their ghastly work.

"The grave of my mother in law, Mrs.
Schwartz, who died about three years
ago, was opened and the body partially
exhumed. Not finding what was wanted
here, the grave was left open to the
elements, and Mr. Barnesley's last resting place was dug up. The skeleton was
dragged out and the left hand separated
at the wrist joint.

"Several days afterwards, judging from
the appearances, my son, while out hunt-
ing, passed through the cemetery and
made the frightful discovery. You can
better imagine our horror and indigna-
tion. The grand jury of Bartow county
is now probing into the matter, and we
shall spare no trouble or expense to
run the foul perpetrators to earth."

After the death of Godfrey Barnesley
his son went to Brazil, and is a man of
wealth and influence there now. Godfrey Barnesley, grandson of the dead
man, spent the summer at his old home.
He is taking a dental course in a Philadelphia college, and is a brilliant young
fellow.

The final, most devastating misfortune occurred in the summer of 1906, when a tornado roared through Barnsley Gardens, destroying a portion of the manor house roof. Barnsley's valuable furnishings were removed from the house for safekeeping, and the Saylors moved their family and servants into the kitchen wing and brandy cellar, until the great manor could be repaired. Saylor soon drafted a plan to rebuild the huge structure, but due to a lack of funds and later, failing health, he was never able to accomplish the task. Shortly thereafter, the great Barnsley Manor began to fall into ruin.

Saylor had proven to be a thoroughly practical and energetic man, but while developing his formulas in the early 1900's, his life became filled with hardships and struggles. And he would never live long enough to see the tremendous growth of the industries he established.

B.F.A. Saylor passed from the scene in 1912, but not before teaching his sons the old Barnsley art of survival, by farming, making whiskey and brandy, and leaving behind for his eldest son, the inherent responsibility of maintaining the estate. Therefore, the final destiny of the family empire would eventually come to rest on Godfrey Barnsley's Great Grandson, "James Preston Saylor." And Preston would never forget the role he was to play in preserving the family estate. Thus is was that Addie Saylor and her children inherited the remainder of Godfrey Barnsley's dream with all its grandeur. But, along with the dream came the never ending burden of controlling and protecting their inheritance from the greedy land tyrants of the day and the rapid changing times of a new south in a new century. Addie's strong willed sons, Preston and Harry, grew up during a period of uncertainty and stagnation in southern culture – fighting and clawing for an existence in a society that had never fully recovered from the Confederate War of Independence. It was an era of bare knuckle prize fighting – bootleg whiskey, the invention of the automobile, Atlanta's own Coca-Cola, and finally the raw hunger of the Great American Depression.

James Preston Saylor was born at Barnsley Gardens on November 8, 1900. Since Addie Saylor was unable to provide the nourishment her healthy son required, he was soon turned over to Aunt "Emma Pritchett", a family servant, and friend, who lovingly nursed him through his adolescence.

From an interview with Emma Pritchett (1870-1960) in 1955 at Kingston, Georgia came the following:

*"Oh yes, I was born and raised over there. And they was my family. Why, I nursed that child, Preston, my own self at the same time I was feeding my baby, Emory. Miss Addie just couldn't get any milk to come foa the baby, so I took care of that child...and kept 'em alive and healthy. Guess I did all right by it, cause that Preston made a big ole healthy boy...(*Emma laughed*) Oh my! I sure would like to see em now...ain't seen that boy in a long time."*

Uncle Ned pushing Emory and Preston with Aunt Emma in the background.

Preston soon grew into a husky boy, extremely advanced for his age, who some had said, was the spitting image of his grandfather Captain Baltzelle. He had proved to be a very intelligent child who, by the tender age of four, had learned to read and write. The Saylor children first attended the Barnsley School on the homestead, and later the Old Cherokee Institute in the town of Adairsville, six miles north of Barnsley Gardens.

From early childhood, Preston had adored his father and often followed him over the estate, taking in the farms, the sawmill and the whiskey stills. He would forever cherish the last moments spent with his father, and his last words of advice that would remain strong in Preston's memory for the rest of his days.

During his teen years, Preston became interested in prize fighting and he and his brother, Harry, set up a practice ring near the barn yards where they would spend their weekends engaging in spar fights with the local boys.

Godfrey Barnsley's Great Grandsons
Preston and Harry Saylor sparring at Woodlands.

By the age of seventeen, Preston had grown into a two hundred-pound hulk of a man with long gorilla arms, a very strong upper torso, and huge leather-like fists. In later years, many of the old timers remembered that "Pres" Saylor could grip a hundred-pound sack of fertilizer under each arm and tote it across the fields.

On the other hand, brother "Harry," eleven months younger, seemed a bit more laid back and opposite in temperament from Preston. Harry, who some had said was the "apple" of his mother's eye, seemed to inherit his features from the Barnsley side of the family, growing into a tall dark haired lad, yet more slender, and not so husky as his brother, Preston. During childhood, Harry had appeared to be more of an inside boy, who preferred spending much of his time at his mother's social gatherings and the like. But, while growing into manhood, Harry and his brother, Preston, had shared at least one thing in common. Both had become deeply overshadowed by their mother's strange spiritual encounters, teaching her sons that her ancestors were constantly watching over them. According to Addie Saylor, Harry was finally converted by one such encounter:

On a cold rainy afternoon in 1918, Harry was summoned to answer a loud knocking on the kitchen door. Just before arriving at the door, he surprisingly discovered his Great Uncle George Barnsley of Brazil smiling at him through a window from the front porch. But, when Harry opened the door to greet Uncle George, he had disappeared. As Harry frantically searched the porch for Uncle George, Addie abruptly exclaimed that it was a message that Uncle George had departed his earthly life. Preston suddenly became angered over the incident, accusing Harry and his mother of wasting precious time on their "ghost" foolishness. But, according to both Addie and Harry, a telegram arrived the next morning stating that Uncle George Barnsley had died in Brazil at the same hour he had appeared in the window the day before. From that time on, it seemed that Harry Saylor, fully supported his mother's spirit communications. But, such encounters continued to aggravate Preston to no end, and would eventually prove to have an intricate effect on the relationship of the brothers.

Preston Saylor was eighteen years old when he informed the overseer, George Sherman, that he was ready to take control of the estate, just as his father had instructed he would do. However, Addie Saylor was not sure her son was fully capable of replacing her loyal overseer who she had greatly depended upon after the death of B.F.A. Saylor. A strong and determined Preston soon confronted his mother on the matter.

(Author's note: From an interview with Preston Saylor in 1957:

"That's when I reminded my mother about the last visit me and Papa had before he died. I still remember every word he said, just like it was yesterday, and he also wrote it in his Will."

"He said to me, son, I know you're still a bit young to understand these kind of things, but I want you to listen closely! You're the oldest, and you're the one that will be responsible for running this place, and taking care of the family later on. It's the way I want it, and just the way your grandmother, Julia, would have wanted it. He said, now I want you and Harry to learn everything you can from Mr. George Sherman, about the farm operation, and as long as I'm able, I'll keep on teaching you how to run the whiskey and brandy stills, cause it will always be a way to help keep the place going. He said, now, you need to be ready for it, cause one day you'll take charge

180

of the place. I'm depending on you!"

"Well, after he died, not a day or night passed that I didn't hear my papa's words running through my mind, and I said, I'd never disappoint em. So that's why I finally told mama I was taking over. I said, we don't need no more outsiders in charge of this place, cause we're the real Barnsley Blood, and with the help of Walt Hammonds, and Uncle "Ned" Phinizy, me and Harry can keep this place going fine. You see, Uncle "Ned" was an old family servant, that knew the place well – he was like a second daddy to me – I loved em, and I knew I could trust em!"

"And then I said to mama, I've got lots of plans, and I'm gonna see em through! I'm gonna fix up the mansion and put things back, just like Grandpa Barnsley had it in the old days – just you watch and see. And, "by jacks," I meant every word of it!")

Uncle Ned holding Preston in 1901

Preston Saylor

PRESTON SAYLOR

The young high-spirited Preston soon became a bit obnoxious concerning his control of the estate that resulted in a bitter confrontation between him and the overseer, George Sherman.

A short time later, George decided to resign his position, and moved his family to a new homestead about a mile west of Barnsley Gardens, leaving Preston to operate the estate. But Addie Saylor would continue to depend on the advice and guidance of George Sherman for some years to come. Preston soon expanded the sawmill operation, and began making larger quantities of whiskey and brandy, that provided extra income. He also spent every moment possible with his favorite past time of spar fighting with his brother, Harry, and the local boys.

It was brother, Harry, who first detected Preston's extraordinary "fighting" talent, and decided he should become a professional prize fighter – to make them rich – and they could operate the family estate, bigger and better than ever.

By 1920, Harry had coaxed Preston into a rigorous training

schedule, setting up regular spar fights that were usually staged under the cool shade of the trees surrounding Godfrey Barnsley's Spring House. Harry would watch with excitement, and grin at his brother's enormous strength as he allowed the local boys to line up and slug Preston in the face and gut as hard as they could in a challenge to put him down. But, Preston had become extremely tough and hardened, and very few were ever able to knock him to his feet. Preston began box fighting in the local towns of Rome, Calhoun, and Dalton, and finally Chattanooga and Atlanta. Harry had anticipated gaining well from the prizefighting venture.

Preston Saylor, the young fighter

Harry Saylor, the promoter

Julia Saylor, sister

After advancing from the barnyard fights at the homestead, on to the Southern Club Fight Circuit, and finally to the bright lights of New York's "Madison Square Gardens," Preston did become the respected pugilist Harry had hoped he would be. But, now he was controlled by big time fight promoters who would no longer need Harry Saylors homespun method of training and managing his brother. Preston was assigned a new management team, and Harry finally returned to the farm, to raise dairy cattle and operate his brother's whiskey and brandy stills, to keep the expensive estate operating. Their sister, Julia, moved to New York to attend the Julliard School of Music and became a musician. She would later settle in Chicago to raise a family.

Due to his extraordinary ability to knock out his opponents early on in the fights, Preston Saylor became known in the roaring twenties fight world as "K.O. Billy Dugan," and finally just, "K.O. Dugan" or "Knock Out Dugan". The huge heavyweight fighter met with such contenders as: Red Baker, Cracker Jack Webb, Gunboat Farley, Yank Gordon, Big Sid Terris, Otto Von Pirate, and many more. By the late 1920's, K.O. Dugan had begun to show the true scars of his profession, an overhung forehead, deep set, dark rimmed eyes, a flat nose protruding across a hard square face, and a voice that was extremely nasal.

K.O. Dugan fought 125 professional bouts and gained a number of victories, but would never be able to give full attention to his colorful career. It was the responsibility of controlling and protecting the family dream at Woodlands that seemed to be a dark cloud hanging over him, thus taking ultimate control of his life. Dugan often frustrated his trainers in the large cities by abruptly returning to Barnsley Gardens between engagements to check on the homestead, plow the fields, work the saw mill, or operate his whiskey stills, and then hurriedly return to the city for the next boxing match. He was sometimes billed as K.O. Dugan, the Georgia farmer.

K.O. Dugan early in his career

During his successful years, he bought fine cars, farm machinery and expensive work mules to be used on the family estate. Dugan was remembered as being quite a colorful character while sporting the countryside in his large custom built Chrysler Imperial Roadster. On one occasion he sent the funds down from New York to rebuild Godfrey Barnsley's Manor, but unfortunately, the funds were misused and the large structure continued to fall into ruin.

During his fighting career, Preston "K.O. Dugan" Saylor was often plagued by dishonest fight promoters, land shysters after the homestead, and finally the loss of a true love. He often argued with his mother and brother, Harry, over their strange spiritual antics that he considered to be a hindrance to the family estate. He was especially angered when he learned that his father's old business attorney had totally swindled his mother by taking over the business, and embezzling most of the stocks left in the company.

Addie with son Harry (1935)

Since prohibition had ruled whiskey making illegal, Dugan was finally forced to face revenuers sent by the Federal Government. In 1927, the notorious murder of a Georgia State Revenue Officer, "Lee Cape" brought on even more pressure. When "Cape's" badly mutilated body was found near Barnsley

Gardens, Dugan was compelled to shut down his illegal distillery. Although he had not been involved in the incident, he was soon plagued with an investigation by Federal authorities just as he had anticipated, and his whiskey earnings came to a sudden halt. Then, on returning from a lengthy boxing tour, K.O. Dugan discovered that his brother was being heavily influenced by a group of outside investors who had convinced Harry that he should be running the estate, and who wanted to become partners with him to get the rich minerals and prime timber on the land. Such persons began to circulate rumors that caused much animosity between the Saylor brothers. The gossip soon traveled that Dugan intended to cheat Harry out of his inheritance, while some told Dugan that when Harry was drunk, he had vowed to get rid of him so that he could take over the estate - the strain was tremendous!

As time passed, the brothers became more at odds and grew further apart. They frequently argued over the estate, their birthrights, and even their women. At the beginning of the Depression, Dugan had courted the beautiful Miss Emily, a local schoolteacher. But when Dugan was away, it was his "charming" brother Harry who stepped in, and proposed marriage to Miss Emily. As it turned out however, neither of the brothers were fortunate enough to win Miss Emily's hand.

Harry tried to convince his family that he had devised a better method of operating the estate by joining forces with a group of wealthy land investors. But, Preston didn't trust them. He was already familiar with their "get rich" schemes, and warned Harry that such investors would only get them indebted and take their land. It was the same kind of land leeches he heard his Papa talk about, and he had never forgotten it. He began to threaten Harry about the company he was keeping, and demanded that he stop them from snooping around on the Barnsley property. As the days passed, the Saylor brothers continued to experience a life of turbulence with one another at Barnsley Gardens.

Eventually K.O. Dugan turned into a paranoid, overbearing, and sometimes vicious individual who trusted no one, and would do almost anything to protect his inheritance.

During the early years of the Depression, "Dugan's" fighting career began to fade, and he returned to Barnsley Gardens to operate the homestead. To earn extra income, he began participating in the local carnival fights throughout North Georgia that usually offered a fifty-dollar purse to anyone that could beat the featured fighter. "Dugan" was many times known to K.O. the carnival's fighter in the first or second round, then quickly collect the purse and return to the farm. He soon joined forces with his boyhood friend, Cobb Green, who assisted him in operating the sawmills, and once again, returned to making whiskey and brandy in spite of the Prohibition law. After all, it was a part of Dugan's upbringing. His family had been brewing such products at Woodlands for more than seventy-five years, and he was not about to stop just because of some law that he considered to be highly political and unreasonable. Besides, the times were hard and he needed the handsome profits it provided to survive the Depression. But, no matter how hard the times got, Dugan had no intention of giving up the family dream. They still had the land – and like his grandmother, Julia, and his grandfather, Captain Baltzelle, Dugan had learned to live off the land.

Preston "K.O. Dugan" Saylor at his sawmill
(Courtesy of Fite H. Casey)

After returning from a trip to Florida in early 1933, Dugan found Harry entertaining a wealthy banker and timber dealer who he considered to be totally untrustworthy. According to one of the farm workers at the scene, Dugan suddenly accused his brother of being two faced and began fighting with him. Harry quickly entered his car and fled away.

A few days later, after Dugan had disagreed with a farm tenant about his ill methods of farming, and then discovered he was taking whiskey from the stills without permission, a fierce argument erupted between them. When the tenant began throwing bricks at him, an angry Dugan fired at the man with a shotgun and sprinkled him heavily with buckshot. Since he had warned him several times about his actions, Dugan proceeded to give the wounded fellow a good lecture about honesty and integrity. He then transported him to a local doctor for treatment, and returned him to his house at Barnsley Gardens. The two soon made peace with one another and no charges were made. But when the news of the incident leaked out, the man's brother was influenced by others to file a warrant for Dugan's arrest. Although no one had witnessed the incident, which could have easily freed him of the charges, Dugan reported to the county sheriff that he had truthfully shot the culprit to punish him for his threats and ill deeds. The court, along with two local medical doctors, decided that K.O. Dugan was "punch drunk" from prize fighting and attempted to prove him insane. When Harry was questioned about his brother's sanity, he stated that he had received several blows from Dugan that was illegal since his brother was a professional pugilist. He also agreed with the doctors that Dugan had received too many punches to the head, and should therefore be placed somewhere for treatment. Harry, along with his associates, later tried to convince his mother of the same, but at first Miss Addie did not want to hear such talk. It was the malicious interference of outsiders that she was concerned about.

Although Dugan had not been examined by a doctor of psychiatry or any other expert of mental health, he was sentenced to the state Mental Institution in 1933. While confined there, he became distraught over what his brother was doing at Woodlands, and more hatred began to build in K.O. Dugan. But after a close observation in the months that followed, doctors at the asylum found him to be reasonably sane, and Dugan became a Trustee of the Institution.

Within a few months he returned to Barnsley Gardens to find that his brother, Harry, had been awarded full control of the estate of which he at first accepted. But, when he learned that the entire homestead had been mortgaged to support a business arrangement with outside investors, he became even more furious. Dugan demanded his share of the profits, but Harry had nothing to give. His business ventures had continued to devour money, and he had used some of the mortgage funds to purchase a new automobile, and a filling station business in Rome, Georgia. Harry had felt sure he was financially safe, since he believed that President Roosevelt's "New Deal" was about to end the Depression and prosperity was just around the corner. He had also been led to believe that his new associates would turn the Barnsley Estate into a lucrative business enterprise. But, the Depression had maintained a harsh grip on the South, and business was still slow. As Harry found himself gradually heading toward a financial crisis, he and his brother began to argue ferociously. After another harsh fight between the two, Harry accused Dugan of harassment and attempted to have him legally forced from the property, and sent back to the asylum. Dugan then left on his own will. Several months later, however, some of his friends discovered he had been living in the outlying barns and farm buildings, while watching his brother's movements. When one of Miss Addie's servants had discovered the fugitive hiding in a barn loft, she began to secretly take him food and water.

During the early morning hours of November 5, 1935, Preston "K.O. Dugan" Saylor appeared suddenly at the rear entrance to the kitchen wing brandy cellar where Harry and his mother had been living during the Depression. He demanded to enter the house and see the business books, and wanted to use the log truck to haul off some of his work mules to get some money. But, a startled Harry refused his brother and once again threatened to have him arrested and sent back to the asylum. Harry had waited a long time to have control of Woodlands and was not about to give it up easily. From an upstairs room, Addie Saylor could hear the gruff mumbling of her son, Preston, as he entered the house, in spite of Harry's protests. Inside the hallway of Godfrey Barnsley's brandy cellar, Dugan suddenly jerked an automatic pistol from his pocket and pointed it toward Harry. Harry ran away quickly, climbing the cellar stairs to the upper level of the house, with an angry Dugan in heavy pursuit. During the chase, Dugan fired several bullets throughout the house, until Harry was finally struck by a single shot into his chest and collapsed into his mother's arms. Harry Saylor met his violent death in the kitchen wing parlor, lying directly beneath a portrait of his Great Grandfather, Godfrey Barnsley.

(Author's note: The bullet holes and bloodstains from that tragic event remain in the historic kitchen wing at Barnsley Gardens.)

After shooting his brother, Dugan left the homestead walking toward the county jail where he turned over his weapon and surrendered to the County Sheriff. In his statement to a newspaper reporter, a nasal voiced "K.O. Dugan" exclaimed:

> *"I shot my brother, but he had it coming! He took advantage of a little trouble I was in and used it against me, to run me away from my own home where I was born and raised. I also heard about all the threats he made against me. By jacks, he had it coming!"*

Harry Saylor was buried in the Barnsley Church Cemetery about a mile from the Gardens. Addie Saylor had not been able to bare the thought of loosing both of her sons, and therefore pleaded for mercy to be shown toward Preston. She had stated that Preston was just not himself, and that she would always love them both. In 1936, Preston "K.O. Dugan" Saylor was sentenced to life in prison for the shooting death of his brother.

1935 Newspaper with Dugan behind bars

(Photo appeared in various newspapers of the Southeast)

(Author's note: I would eventually conduct many interviews with persons who were involved in the lives and times of the Saylor Brothers. The following came from a compilation of interviews conducted with W.H. Lanham, Frank "Cobb" Green, J.T. Long, and Jess Taylor at Taylor's Store in Halls (Mill) Station in 1957):

Jess Taylor

"That was a mighty bad thing that finally happened between those boys. It broke my heart, cause I loved 'em both. But, now, let me tell you something son – there's two sides to that story! Yes sir! Now, it's true that old Dugan could be mean as a snake if you got 'em all stirred up...but, now everything wasn't Dugan's fault. No sir! Harry was responsible for some of it too, and to tell you the truth, sometimes Harry could be just a little bit on the sneaky side when it came to dealing with his brother."

"My daddy operated the big store across the road there in those days, and the Saylors always traded with him, and the boys hung around there a lot. Later on when Preston got to be known as K.O. Dugan, and was gone off prize fighting, I remember that Harry and Miss Addie would run up some pretty stiff credit on the store books, and they would get behind on paying for it. But, my dad always knew that Preston would take care of it. Yes sir, when Old Dugan came through, he'd stop in and ask my daddy how much they owed and he'd pay up the bill. You could always depend on him!"

"Well, you see, those boys had a lot of outside interference from people toting tales, and stirring up trouble between them. And, to tell you the truth, some of them were trying to get their hands on that land over there that was still rich in bauxite ore and had some of the finest virgin timber you ever laid eyes on. Dugan used to say one of them was an old rich banker and lawyer that had worked for his Papa back in earlier days, the same scoundrel that had cheated Miss Addie out of some business stock. Ole Dugan didn't trust that man one little bit. No sir! Well, anyway, when Dugan was gone off prize fightin' such folks would visit with Harry and tell 'em how he ought to be managing the place instead of his brother – or how they could make 'em rich if he and Miss Addie would join forces with 'em and all such talk as that. Well, you see, Harry got to chummin with 'em a little bit, and Dugan got pretty mad about it, and accused Harry of undermining him. And of course I think Harry wanted to prove he could run the place better than his brother. They never did get along with each other much after that, and as time went on, it seemed like more and more people tried to stir up trouble between them."

Jess Taylor

"Of course now, Harry was a pretty likable boy when .we were growing up, and we had fun together. But, as he got older, it seemed like he turned into sort of a loner. Got to where he wouldn't say much – you know, sort of stayed in his own world and you couldn't really tell what he had *on his mind. But, on the other hand, Old Dugan always seemed to be up front with everything. If he saw you on the street, he would grin and holler at you, no matter how rich or poor you were, and he didn't care who liked it, or didn't like it."*

Frank Green and J.T. Long

"Dugan's main problem was when he caught people double crossing him, he'd try to handle it all by himself with his fist or a pistol, instead of getting himself a lawyer, and trying to handle it legally. And sometimes, he could get pretty mean about things. Of course, Ole Dugan had a lots on 'em, in those days, with that big place hanging over his head and being a prizefighter and everything. And, he had worked dum hard for years on the place. But you see, he felt like Harry wanted him out of the way, and he didn't trust him. But he didn't intend on giving it up. He loved the place and he was going to run things again, his way, no matter who liked it. Why, that boy might have been heavyweight champ of the world if he hadn't had that place hanging over 'em. Cause Old Dugan was strong as a bull, and he could knock 'em out! Yeah boy, he could knock 'em out!"

After Harry's death, Addie Saylor found herself deeply burdened with the mortgage against the Estate. She tried to farm the land with sharecroppers and was finally forced to sell some of the family heirlooms to keep the debtors from closing in. Her closest companion was her grandson, Clarence Simms, the son of her daughter, Julia, who lived in Chicago. But, at the outbreak of World War II, Clarence was drafted into the Army leaving Miss Addie all alone. Addie had now become a tired and lonely old lady living among her mixed memories. Her only solace seemed to be the letters she received from her son, Preston, at Tattnal State Prison, and the lonely sounds of Harry's footsteps that she claimed to hear each night coming up the old cellar stairs.

In 1941, Addie made an attempt to get her son, Preston, released from prison so he could help her save the homestead. During an interview with a newspaper reporter she stated:

> *"I need Preston now. He has always been a wonderful hand on the place, and he could get things going here again. He is doing so good at the State Prison and writes me regularly – Preston didn't do that awful deed alone. If only the people who were responsible could be made to pay...the people who egged them on...the people who carried the lies."*

But, Preston would not be released in time to rescue the Estate. Addie Saylor died on June 7, 1942, leaving Barnsley Gardens heavily in debt. She was buried beside her son, Harry, at the Barnsley Methodist Church, a mile from the Gardens. A few months later, the estate administrator ordered the last 1,725 acres of Barnsley Gardens, and all of its furnishings to be sold at public auction.

CHAPTER 12

THE FINALE

On a beautiful autumn day in 1942, the singsong chant of an auctioneer echoed loudly from Godfrey Barnsley's Prominent Hill. From his lofty perch overlooking the boxwood terrace of Barnsley Manor, he eagerly hammered down bids for its fabulous relics. Literally hundreds of priceless heirlooms from the four corners of the world, and some of the finest tracts of land in the South were being offered up and sold to the high bidders.

The crowds had gathered in from the local towns and from Atlanta, Chattanooga, and even as far away as Savannah to attend the extraordinary event. Some were wealthy merchants and collectors who had come strictly in pursuit of the valuable "Barnsley" antique treasures, while others were just old friends or former residents who only came to bid their last good-byes to a grand estate they had grown to love and respect. It was the place where their families had lived, and worked, and the land they had depended on for survival through the years.

Some of them eventually drifted away from the auction, searching the grounds, hoping to retrieve at least one final souvenir from the great Woodlands Plantation. They were soon collecting bits of foliage from the rare Asian Cunningemia and gathering up small fragments of the crumbling statuary in the old water cascade.

An hour later, inside the formal gardens, two of the city merchants were admiring Miss Julia's Italian marble fountain, and swapping tales of her legendary ghost. Then on suddenly catching sight of the auctioneer offering up the huge "Queen Marie Antoinette" golden clock, they rushed from the gardens to cast their bids on the famous heirloom.

Meanwhile, down on the main road winding through the valley below, a thick cloud of dust swirled from the wheels of a dark sedan, speeding toward the Woodlands' gates. The car soon careened from the road roaring through the gates, until finally coming to a halt on the hillside barely fifty yards below the auction tent. Before the dust could chance to settle, an attractive middle aged couple emerged from the car. For a moment they paused, listening to the auctioneer's saddening drone of finality bellowing over their heads, then hurriedly climbed the long flight of steps leading to the peak of the prominent hill. Julia Saylor Paulis, the last hereditary mistress of Woodlands and her Northern born husband had arrived late from Chicago to attend the final liquidation of the family estate. Clasping her husband's hand at arms length behind her, an anxious Julia moved swiftly ahead, through the hundreds of furnishings strewn helter-skelter over the grounds, only to discover an incredible nightmare unfolding before her eyes. A careless crowd of spectators were trampling through Godfrey Barnsley's Manor, plucking rare plants at their leisure, and plundering through four generations of family keepsakes.

Julia had known that such a day would come, but never had she expected to witness such treatment of the old homestead. Neither had she prepared herself to watch personal family photographs, clothing and toys from her childhood actually being offered up to strangers for only pennies of their value.

As the stunned couple continued to move slowly through the upheaval, watching the bidders and occasionally greeting old friends from the past, Julia would soon make another heart breaking discovery. Almost hidden behind a long row of the

Barnsley "Purple Black Rose" stood a large collection of original family portraits, waiting their turn to be offered up on the auction block. In frozen silence, Julia studied the long line of her "Woodlands" ancestors, vividly recalling both the triumphs and misfortunes that had befallen them all.

A beautiful oil on canvas had so elegantly depicted Godfrey Barnsley and his beloved Julia, the handsome couple who had started it all. Next was a large pastel of her own dear mother, Addie who had fought to the end to hold on to the dream. A little further along the path, she could see the old family servant, 'Uncle Ned,' smiling softly from a large oval faded with age. Julia glared helplessly at Uncle Ned, then returned his smile. Moments later, tears began to well in her eyes and she sobbed, while staring into the perfect likeness of her two brothers' portraits resting in the dirt alongside the old kitchen wing porch. Her pale frustrated features seemed to tell all as she lifted their portraits to the edge of the porch and sat down beside them. While gently rubbing her fingers over the paintings, Julia appeared for a moment to drift into a subconscious state of mind, totally separated from all her physical surroundings. No longer could she seem to hear the shrill cry of the auctioneer, or feel the presence of the restless crowds toting away her precious Woodlands. But then, on suddenly being alerted by her husband that people were staring at the last of the notorious Barnsley kin, she proudly lifted her chin, and once again came to her senses. And once again, Julia remembered, it had been the ill fate of her strong willed brothers that had brought her down to that very day – the day that Godfrey Barnsley's dream would succumb to the mere mercy of auctioneer's gavel and the Barnsleys at Woodlands would be no more.

(Author's note: According to eye witnesses on that afternoon in 1942, Julia Saylor Paulis plucked one last specimen of her favorite "Rose" from the gardens and left Woodlands forever. Julia remained with her family in Chicago until her death in 1965.)

Preston "K.O. Dugan" Saylor was released from prison in 1943. He soon began a new life in a small town near Atlanta, Georgia, where he would prove to be a successful and well respected businessman for many years. "K.O. Dugan" died in his sleep at Macon, Georgia, in 1986.)

An older K. O. Dugan
(1955)

Julia Saylor
(in later life)

At the time of the foreclosure auction in 1942, the last 1,725 acres of Barnsley land was sold to Mr. and Mrs. G.C. Phillips of Birmingham, Alabama, who were also the high bidders for several of the Barnsley heirlooms. But, the majority of the valuable collection of fine furniture, art, china and imported statuary was sold to various individuals, so that many of the Barnsley artifacts eventually became scattered throughout the Southeast. By 1954, the Estate had dwindled to 1,200 acres, and was sold to Earl McCleskey of Alpharetta, Georgia. A few years later, the McCleskeys moved into the historic kitchen wing and began establishing a cattle and poultry farm on the property. At first, McCleskey made every effort to maintain the historic area and allowed occasional visitors to view the gardens. But, as time passed, vandals and souvenir hunters began stalking the grounds, and the Estate was soon fenced off and locked away from the outside world. Within a few years, wild vegetation had taken over the buildings and gardens.

For the next forty years, Barnsley Gardens at Woodlands would lie dormant in its own wilderness with a modern world growing up around it. A generation passed and another one came until finally only a few of the local residents remembered the once fabulous Barnsley Gardens.

(Author's note: After spending some thirty years researching and collecting memorabilia on four generations of the Barnsleys, I knew, without a doubt that Barnsley Gardens was one of the most fascinating landmarks of Antebellum America. Since the late 1940's, I had sadly witnessed the deterioration of its historic buildings and gardens, and longed to see it restored to its former glory. Although I had wholeheartedly encouraged its owners to allow such a restoration, several attempts to purchase and restore the property had proved unsuccessful. By the mid 1980's, much to my regret, Barnsley Gardens at Woodlands had almost faded into oblivion.

Never the less, the Barnsley story was not ready to end. In due time, Godfrey Barnsley's illustrious dream would experience a transcendent awakening.)

A DREAM COMES TRUE

By the late 1980's, most of Earl McCleskey's family had grown up and moved away, and he found managing the estate alone to be a tremendous task. In 1987, he decided to sell historic Barnsley Gardens. By that time, most of the historic Barnsley structures were overgrown with heavy layers of kudzu vines, thick masses of underbrush and rambling vines of wisteria. A thicket of wild trees had grown up in the interior of the huge manor ruins and the great brick walls had begun to crumble. The rare English Boxwood inside the massive parterre were snarled and twisted, and also choked out with wild trees and other debris. The garden ponds were filled with muck, and the overseer quarters and spring house in the old village compound had all but fallen in.

An Overgrown Barnsley Gardens - 1988

(Photography by Oscar Coker)

The Manor Ruins

Front Entrance to the Manor

Interior of Manor

Spring House

The destiny of Godfrey Barnsley's Woodlands indeed looked very bleak until the year 1988, when suddenly a miraculous event occurred. At that time, Carl Cofer, an attorney for the Atlanta based investment company of Prince Hubertus Fugger, and his wife, Princess Alexandra, of Augsburg, Germany, traveled to Barnsley Gardens to view the property as a possible land investment. A binder was soon placed on the property and a few weeks later, the Fuggers arrived from Germany to negotiate the final purchase of the remaining 1,154 acres of the Barnsley Estate.

(Author's note: I immediately met with Prince Fugger to explain the estate's historical value and to present him with some of the original Barnsley documents and photographs I had collected over the years. After finally relating to him some of the treasured Barnsley stories, I was delighted to see that he was becoming caught up in the historic fascination of Barnsley Gardens. He soon announced that the unique estate should, and would, be preserved. Due to the foresight and the investment of Prince Fugger, the restoration of Barnsley Gardens at Woodlands had become a reality. My life long dream had finally come true. I was requested to be the historical advisor/curator of Barnsley Gardens, and we were soon engaged in excavating its history from beneath fifty years of neglect.)

CHAPTER 13

THE RESTORATION

First, the clean up operation of Barnsley Gardens, directed by the Estate caretaker, Bobby McElwee, proved to be a tremendous undertaking, even with the use of modern machinery. One of the first tasks was to cut and clear up the hundreds of wild trees that had grown up in the old stage coach road, leading into the property. This was accomplished by a crew of workmen under the direction of George Adams, who had grown up near the Gardens, and was delighted to take part in the restoration project.

Next was the job of excavating the 1840's overseer/coach house, the commissary, and the original Woodlands post office, from beneath mountains of kudzu and wisteria vines that had woven their way into the very woodwork of the buildings. This was accomplished by Brent Coker and other volunteers. Local preservation carpenters were hired to replace the rotted flooring and porches that had fallen from the structures.

A short time later, we removed the large trees that had grown up in the Manor ruins. Many hours were spent carefully cutting away each tree to prevent further damage to the building. Brick masons, under the direction of Bill Corey, began repairing the handmade brick walls and crumbling arches of the mammoth structure. A preservation study conducted by the Rome Area Heritage Foundation proved to be very helpful in re-stabilizing the Manor. Once the trees were removed, the grounds were excavated and new floors were installed.

George Adams clearing old stage road

Clent Coker Clearing Ground at the Manor

The Commissary Before

After

Overseer, Coach House, and Post Office (Before)

(After)

With the assistance of Greg and Brent Coker, we soon began renovating the historic kitchen wing by uncovering the original floors and stripping away a century and a half of paint from the walls and the woodwork. Since I had long envisioned a family museum in the kitchen wing, it was there I began placing many of the historic Barnsley photographs and other items I had collected over the years. (Two years later, with the assistance of Bobby McEllwee, Bete Avanti, and Sep Murray, I would convert the historic kitchen wing into the Barnsley Gardens museum.)

As the crews continued clearing and restoring the prominent hill, they were instructed to carefully collect and document every fragment of Barnsley history excavated from the grounds around the historic structures. In the months to follow, I would receive many interesting items of historic value.

Through the years of researching original war documents and family letters, I had learned of the basic locations of soldier encampments on the Estate during the war between the States. I therefore, engaged two professional civil war historians, Herbert Ortwine and Gilbert Smith, to comb through the old campgrounds on the property. Within a few months, almost three hundred fragments from General Sherman's Atlanta campaign were excavated from the hills surrounding Barnsley Gardens, thus further documenting the Estate's involvement in that crucial event of American History. I would also receive much assistance from two of my old friends, the noted Civil War specialists, Ron Casey and Larry Mealor, who had spent many years excavating the battle fields of North Georgia. They would later provide me an invaluable collection of Civil War artifacts for the Barnsley Museum. Others who furnished artifacts and information from the War Era were Ed Byers, Buddy and Eunice Autry, Jones Layton, John Roegge, Dyan Nelson, Vernon Ayers and Harold McCoy.

The Barnsley Family Cemetery lying in the woods about

two hundred yards southeast of the Manor had also turned into a forest of trees and undergrowth. It was soon cleaned up and plans were made to replace some of the grave stones. The cemetery contained about forty-eight graves of the Barnsley families and their servants. Due to the financial hardships at the time of Godfrey's death, he had requested that no stone was to be placed on his grave. He had felt it would be of no real benefit, and preferred that all funds be spent on the "living" at Woodlands. But, in 1989, with the aid of Prince Fugger and the descendants of Dr. George S. Barnsley, I was able to design an appropriate marker and place it over his grave. But, there was yet another grave on the property to be cleaned up and manicured. It was the grave of Confederate Col. Richard G. Earle of the Second Alabama Calvary who had given his life to protect the Barnsleys during the summer of 1864.

Kitchen Wing Under Renovation

Rear View of Kitchen Wing 1989

Godfrey's Grave

Planning the Renovation of Col. Earle's Grave (1988)

One day when I was sorting through some of my old photographs of the Barnsley's, I was suddenly struck with an idea. Wouldn't it be great to have the Barnsley family descendents return to Woodlands for a grand reunion? It would not only be good publicity, but also an honorable way for the Barnsley's to participate in supporting the restoration project we had undertook. Prince Fugger liked the idea, so I began organizing the event in the spring of 1989. With the assistance of two dear friends, Ila Green McStotts, who had grown up near the gardens, and Carolyn Black Hill, a local public relations director, the reunion took place in October, 1989. Godfrey Barnsley's descendents from three countries attended the three-day event that resulted in a most memorable occasion.

It was during the reunion that some of the descendents through Dr. George Barnsley, from Brazil and California, presented me with additional artifacts that I would eventually place in the Barnsley museum. They were: Harold Barnsley Holland, Julia Holland McDonell, Robert Barnsley Holland and Mary Holland Grizzle. Later I would also receive some interesting items from Dr. Paulo Pessoa, and Jorge Barnsley Pessoa, descendents of Lucien Barnsley in South America.

A Family Gathering at the Manor - 1880's

The family descendants regathered at the manor more than a hundred years later (Reunion of 1989)

(Photos by Bill Owens)

The Author at reunion, with members
of the Barnsley Family

It was in 1989, that Prince Fugger and his legal advisor began searching for a trained horticulturist to supervise the restoration of the historic gardens. They had hoped to find someone who would be "hands on" with their training and experienced in restoring the grounds. Steve Wheaton, a graduate from the University of Vermont with a major degree in horticulture, turned out to be just that kind of person. When Steve first visited Barnsley Gardens in 1989, he was immediately fascinated with finding an original "Downing Style Gardens" nestled away in the wooded hills of Northwest Georgia. He was very familiar with the works of the noted "Andrew Jackson Downing" since he had grown up near the Hudson River Valley of New York State where many of the Downing style country landscapes had been preserved. Steve had also studied and researched the unique Downingesque concepts while in college. After viewing the badly overgrown landscape at Barnsley Gardens, he considered it a wonderful challenge to become involved in its restoration.

In January of 1990, Steve Wheaton became the horticulturist of Barnsley Gardens at Woodlands. His research assistant was also a skilled horticulturist, from Swarthemore College in Pennsylvania by the name of Erica Glasenor.

Steve soon went to work, handling much of the manual labor himself to resurrect as many of the original gardens as he possibly could.

In order to assist Steve and his labor assistant, Keith Reeves, with the authentic restoration, I began searching through the many Barnsley letters and receipts I had collected over the years, to uncover every possible document pertaining to the historical gardens and buildings. Additional documentation pertaining to the gardens was also found in the archives of Emory University and in the University of Georgia. Also, the works of horticulturist, Catherine M. Howett pertaining to the "Downingesque" setting at Woodlands proved to be helpful.

First of all, the massive boxwood Parterre lying directly in front of the Manor ruins was carefully cleared of its entanglement of briars and volunteer trees, slowly removing each stump so as not to damage any of the original boxwood. Since the huge overgrown shrubs had been standing for a century and a half, much patience and care was used in trimming them back to the desired size, for fear of them going into shock, and losing them. They were first pruned back about a third, so as to allow the lower branches to sprout new growth. Annual pruning would then follow until they could be reduced to the normal size they were kept during the Nineteenth Century.

The original circular basin beneath the fountain in the center of the Parterre was soon excavated and found to be in fairly good condition. But, the remainder of the marble fountain itself had been removed after the auction in 1942, and its new owner, who had refurbished the fountain, did not want to part with it. He did, however, allow the Gardens' restoration staff to view and study it as a guide for molding a new one. It was from that study, along with old photographs I had collected, that Prince Fugger commissioned an Atlanta sculptor, Christine Sibley to construct a new fountain. A slight modification was made in the final construction, by adding a molded replica of the face of Julia Barnsley to replace one of the lion heads on the base of the fountain. It was felt that such a change would be well fitting, since it was for Julia the original Gardens had been planned.

Formal Gardens (before)

Formal Gardens and Fountain (after)

The Restored Ruins and Gardens (1990's)

A story telling event at the Manor Ruins
(After restoration)

The serpentine walks leading through the geometrically designed Parterre were resurfaced with creek stone and the border beds filled with original type plants and heirloom roses.

Since Barnsley Gardens was once considered a rose showcase of the South, the Fugger family had wanted it to remain true to the tradition. Therefore, Steve Wheaton and his crew began searching out all of the original roses that had grown wild on the property, carefully pruning and nurturing them back to health. In 1991, after studying the original list of roses mentioned in Barnsley's ledgers, Steve drove to Michael Shoups "Antique Rose Emporium" in Houston, Texas, and purchased one hundred varieties of heirloom roses to be planted at the Gardens. Also, the owners of other historic homesteads in the area offered additional roses and heirloom plants that were originally collected from Woodlands.

(Author's note: "It was certainly a pleasure for me to travel with Steve to some of the old places, and share in the excitement of digging them up and returning them to Godfrey Barnsley's original Gardens.")

From the Barnsley Rose Collection:
(Photography by Alexandra Fugger)

By 1970, the left wing cottage standing on the upper rear terrace to the south side of the Great Manor had been torn down, thus, leaving a large open space where the "Rose Tea Garden" had once stood. The yard was soon leveled and sown with grass by the horticulture crew. Jane Bath of Stone Mountain, Georgia designed a broad perennial border to enclose the entire rear terrace. Dan Franklin, an Atlanta landscape architect, directed the building of a large wooden arbor that was constructed on the south end of the rear terrace overlooking the lower Woodlands Bog Gardens. Old fashioned clematis vines, along with the "Fugger's" favorite rose, "New Dawn," were planted to cover the arbor. A smaller boxwood Parterre that had been standing on the south side of the Manor since the 1850's had grown out of control and was beyond salvaging. Prince Fugger, therefore, decided to have it cleared and replaced with new boxwood, and heirloom roses. It soon became known as the "Fugger Parterre."

Once the formal gardens had been restored, Wheaton and his crew began working to rescue the long overgrown Gardens in the lower Woodlands. First was the large spring fed Bog Gardens and the old water cascade lying deep in the valley, a hundred yards to the south of the prominent hill. A very careful excavation project was soon put into motion to determine the general layout of original paths, water features and planning areas. When the decaying trees and stumps, along with a half-century of washed in dirt and debris were removed, Carl Cofer suddenly discovered a brick surface buried under two feet of soil. As the excavation continued, it turned out to be a brick floored swale opening into a deep channel winding through the "Bog" Gardens until finally returning to the Barnsley Creek. He had discovered a very practical drainage system for the lower Gardens, built 150 years earlier by Godfrey Barnsley. Once the bog was cleaned out and reshaped, many rare plants, including a variety of water lilies were set out through the area. On the steep slope between the lower bog and the Manor Ruins, more than 50,000 daffodils were planted.

The Arbor

Perennial Bed

Lower Bog

(Photography by Alexandra Fugger)

Just over the next wooded terrace, a hundred yards south of the water bog, was a second spring fed pond that was called the Oriental Pond. Although it was filled with a hundred years of sediment, the original brick dam holding the pond was still intact. A large wooden plug designed to regulate the flow of water through the dam, was also still intact. The cleaning and restoration of the pond turned out to be quite a menial task since all the muck and debris had to be removed by hand until the water was again deep and clear.

(Author's note: According to notes I had found in the daily record book of Dr. George S. Barnsley, he had completed the dam on April 14, 1860, to provide a water reservoir for new brandy stills he had erected nearby.)

Since both the Barnsleys and the Fuggers had been very fond of rhododendrons, over 400 plants, boasting some twenty varieties, were planted on a huge rounding hill above the water bog and the Oriental Pond. Also many heirloom camellias were set out among the rhododendrons that contributed greatly to the colorful grandeur of the lower Woodlands. By this time, it was evident that Godfrey's wilderness Eden was gradually returning to its former splendor.

Rhododendrons and Camellias

THE OPENING

Barnsley Gardens and its museum was opened as a public historic attraction in the fall of 1991, although the renovation of the Estate would continue for years to come.

At that time, the horticulturist, Steve Wheaton, and Clent Coker the Historian, began traveling throughout the State to promote the opening of the Gardens. Many interviews were held with the news media, and lectures conducted with garden and civic organizations to promote the outstanding historic and horticultural value of the Estate.

In the spring of 1992, a dedicated staff of local volunteers began assisting with the general operation of the historical area. As time progressed, history buffs and lovers of horticulture became totally charmed with the very essence of Barnsley Gardens.

As the visitors continued to gain in number, it was decided that a fine restaurant on the property would be a must in order for the Gardens to fully succeed. It was, therefore, in 1993, that Prince Fugger commissioned Clent Coker to begin searching for a historic building that could be moved to the Gardens and renovated into a Southern cuisine restaurant. It was also decided that if enough historic buildings of the area could be moved to the property, it would be a great way of reproducing the original 1800's Woodlands Village while also preserving more of the colorful history of Northwest Georgia.

(Author's note: After spending several months meeting with the owners of historic houses that I had researched in the area, I met with Civil War historian, Gilbert Smith, about the historic Rice House in Floyd County near Rome, Georgia. The unique structure had been built in 1854, by Fleming Rice, a well-known wheat planter of the area. Smith had conducted a thorough study of the house and was very familiar with its history, especially pertaining to the role it played in the War Between the States. An important battle had taken place in front of the house in 1864, and bullet holes from that battle were still visible on the exterior walls of the old structure. After visiting the house, Prince Fugger and myself decided it had great potential to become the historic style restaurant we had hoped for at Barnsley Gardens. I soon met with the descendants of Fleming Rice of New York City, who owned the property, and within a few months, was able to negotiate its purchase. A short time later, I joined with a moving contractor to study the structure and determine the most feasible method of moving it to the Gardens. The removal turned out to be an overwhelming project that required endless hours of deliberating over every detail to ensure the least liability of damage. The two-story structure was soon disassembled into four sections for safe removal. Since we had wanted the house to remain as authentic as possible, I was careful to see that each board, window and door removed from the building was numbered and protected, in order to be replaced in the same manner. With the assistance of historic photographer "Bill Owen," I was able to pictorially document each facet of the removal.)

It was in the early Spring of 1994, that the historic Rice House arrived at its new location, on a beautifully landscaped hill about 150 yards northeast of Godfrey Barnsley's Manor. The next nine months were spent reassembling the house while adding an ultra modern kitchen, walk-in coolers, and a wine cellar to accommodate the guests. A variety of shrubs, southern magnolias and heirloom roses, along with an old-fashioned herb garden added greatly to the surrounding landscape. The Barnsley Gardens Restaurant, featuring old Southern cuisine, staged its opening in the spring of 1995. It soon became very busy with, not only daily guests, but also for catering large weddings and other special functions at the Gardens.

The Removal of Historic Rice House
(Photos by Clent Coker and Bill Owens)

Rice House Restaurant at Barnsley Gardens

In 1993, the historic "Adair House" of Taylorsville, Georgia (c. 1863), was also disassembled and moved to Barnsley Gardens. Its owner, Ricky L. Woods, had donated the structure for historic preservation. The large "Planter Style" house with its detached kitchen wing would later be renovated to accommodate the administrative offices at Barnsley Gardens. The building was placed at the end of a long meadow directly west of the main entrance to the Gardens.

It was during the same time period that Prince Fugger's attorney, Carl Cofer, located an 1830's log structure in Central Georgia that was also moved to the Gardens. The uniquely constructed "Cabin" was placed near the rear exit gates to become the Barnsley Plant Shop.

(Author's notes: Since my childhood, I had kept a keen eye on the historic "Penn House," a very rare 1820's log structure near Adairsville, only hoping that it would be preserved. It was in 1993, that I finally purchased the house, with plans of restoring it. However, Prince Fugger had also expressed to me his desire to restore such a cabin that could be used as his personal residence during his visits to the Gardens. I therefore arranged for him to purchase the house and had it moved to a secluded portion of the property where it was eventually restored to its original state.

Another early house in the area that I had wanted to preserve was the 1840's "Pioneer Cabin" of Jeptha and Nancy Green standing near Halls Mill, about two miles from the Gardens. The family of James David Green (1867-1952) who was born in the cabin, had been dear friends to my family. I could also remember the stories Mr. Green told during my childhood about living in the old house and growing up near Barnsley Gardens. Although, some of the house had fallen into ruin, I was finally able to purchase it for the Gardens in 1994, thus, salvaging one more segment of the colorful Bartow County History. The old hand hewn structure was reassembled near the larger "Penn" cabin, to become a storage and carriage shed.

It was also in 1994, that I was able to save the remainder of the William Collins' cabin that had been standing in the northeast portion of the county since about 1810. Earlier, I had found in the house the family register that included the history of the structure, along with papers left behind by Union soldiers who had used the grounds as a campsite in 1864. The huge logs were soon moved to the Gardens where they still await reconstruction.

Another house in the historic complex at Barnsley Gardens was the outer shell of an 1880's farm house that was left standing since it had some historic significance of its own. During the early 1900's, the family of "Charlie Floyd" had resided two years in the house. A short time later, the family moved to Oklahoma, and young "Charlie" (born near Adairsville, Georgia) became the notorious "Pretty Boy Floyd."

By the mid 1990's, Barnsley Gardens was hosting many thousands of visitors each year. We soon arranged for a series of special events to be held at the gardens. They included an annual daffodil festival, an antique quilt show, Civil War reenactments, and a Barnsley story telling event that provided much entertainment for the guests.

By the close of 1996, however, the cost of maintaining the estate proved to be so tremendous that it was decided the gardens needed additional attractions to make them more profitable.

Therefore, in 1997, a new plan was put into motion to build an 18-hole championship golf course that would take in almost four hundred acres of the lush meadows and beautiful wooded hills on the Barnsley Estate.

The plan also called for an 1800's "Downing" style village, complete with its own gardens, that would be keeping in true harmony with the original concepts of Godfrey Barnsley and Andrew Jackson Downing. It would be a completely different type of resort with a very relaxed country atmosphere – and the only "Downing" style resort in the South.

It was in the early spring of 1998, that construction began on the "Barnsley Inn & Golf Resort" at Barnsley Gardens. After following the original "Downing" manuals as the guide for blending the old with the new, the opening of the unique resort in 1999, proved to be well accepted and was a grand success. Now it seems that its past, present, and future all come together in perfect harmony as the Illustrious Barnsley Dream lives on, into the 21st century.

Downing Style Village
at Barnsley Inn & Golf (1999)

Appendix A

Woodlands, Home of ST. ELMO

It has long been a tradition among the residents of Woodlands that Augusta J. Evans Wilson, the author of the famous novel ST. ELMO, did use the Barnsley estate as the setting for her book and that Godfrey's son, George S. Barnsley, was indeed her immortal "St. Elmo".

The prominent novelist from Mobile, Alabama released her first publication of ST. ELMO in 1866. It became one of the best sellers of the 19th Century. New releases were issued as late as 1921.

During the 1850's, while attending a ball for the business elite of the Mobile waterfront, Mrs. Wilson became acquainted with Godfrey Barnsley and his associates. After learning of his magnificent estate being erected on the North Georgia frontier, she was determined to pay a visit. Mrs. Wilson signed the guest register several times throughout the 1860's. She later became so taken by the unparalleled beauty of Godfrey's wilderness "Eden" that she was compelled to use it as the country manor setting in ST. Elmo, which she named "Le Bocage." Le Bocage is the French equivalent of Woodlands. She described the setting as follows:

> *"The furniture throughout the mansion house was elegant and costly; pictures, statues, bronzes, marble, silver, rosewood, ebony, mosaics, satin,*

velvet, naught that the most fastidious and cultivated taste and dilettantism could suggest, or lavish expenditure supply, was wanting; while the elaborate and beautiful arrangement of the extensive grounds showed with how prodigal a hand the owner squandered a princely fortune. The flower garden and lawn comprised fifteen acres, and the subdivisions were formed entirely by hedges, save that portion of the park surrounded by a tall iron railing, where congregated a motley menagerie of deer, bison, a Lapland reindeer, a Peruvian llama, come cashmere goats, a chamois, wounded and caught on the Jungfrau, and a large white cow from Ava. This part of the enclosure was thickly studded with large oaks, groups of beech and elm, and a few enormous cedars which would not have shamed their sacred prototypes sighing in Syrian breezes along the rocky gorges of Lebanon. Here and there, on the soft, green sward, was presented that vegetable antithesis, a circlet of martinet poplars standing vis-a-vis to a clump of willows whose long hair threw quivering, fringe shadows when the slanting rays of dying sunlight burnished the white and purple petals nestling among the clover tufts. Rustic seats of bark, cane, and metal were scattered through the grounds, and where the well-trimmed numerous hedges divided the parterre, china, marble and iron vases of varied mould, held rare creepers and lovely exotics; and rich masses of roses swung their fragrant chalices of crimson and gold, rivaling the glory of Paestum and of Bendemer."

Woodlands, with its gardens and furnishings were truly unique in comparison to other estates of the old south. There is no doubt, the literal illustrations in ST. ELMO describe the true setting of Woodlands at the outset of the Civil War, at a time when George S. Barnsley was, in fact, the manager of his father's estate. (1858-1861)

According to early historians, it was a half century later that the young Atlanta newspaper writer, Mrs. John Marsh, or "Margaret Mitchell," read the classic, ST. ELMO and requested that a friend take her to visit Godfrey Barnsley's Woodlands. Historians, Robert White and Joe Mahan, remembered that the writer was overwhelmed with the rich stories of Addie Saylor, relating to the hardships of her mother, Julia, during the Civil War. Consequently, some years later, in Mitchell's *Gone With the Wind,* many parallels became evident between Julia's life at Woodlands and the tenacious "Scarlett" of Tara Plantation. The invading and looting of the Union Army, the lumber dealer, Captain Baltzelle, and the wealthy blockade runner, Baron Von Schwartz, along with Julia's hunger and slaving in the fields, were all present in Mitchell's masterpiece. Some excerpts from Julia's memoirs, and the dark hero typified in *"St. Elmo,"* also showed up in the book. It then seemed evident that Julia's life at Woodlands had become one of the great inspirations for *"Gone With the Wind."*

(Author's note: During the 1960's, the original Woodlands guest registers signifying the visits of such distinguished guests, were still in the possession of Mrs. G.C. Phillips in Kingston, Georgia. They were reviewed by historians, Joe Mahan, Vernon Ayers, Robert White and myself. On the death of Mrs. Phillips, they were distributed to various individuals and organizations, some of which have become unknown. They are still being pursued.

Appendix B

THE FUGGER FAMILY

The name "Fugger" has been well known throughout Germany for more than six hundred years. Since the Fuggers were powerful merchants and bankers who loaned money to kings, emperors and popes, and also financed some of Europe's wars, the name has long been associated with great wealth.

The Fugger family was founded early in the 14th Century by Han Fugger, a weaver and farmer. He lived in Graben, near Augsburg, Germany. His son, Johann, became a citizen of Augsburg in 1370, and became a member of the Council of Twelve of the Guild of Weavers, becoming prosperous in his cloth trade there. Johann died in 1408, leaving a large fortune to his sons, Andreas and Jakob, who continued to expand their father's business. They became the heads of two Fugger houses, The Roe Fuggers and the Lily Fuggers. The Roe Fuggers were at first prosperous but then died out.

Jakob respectfully became the head of the Lily Fuggers, (so named because of the Lily appearing in their coat of arms). He had three sons, Ulrich, George and Jakob, who inherited the family business and added to its wealth. They made large loans to the German ruler, Maximillian I, who rewarded them with land and other privileges, including the rank of nobility.

Ulrich Fugger (1441-1510) acted as banker for the

Habsburg Dynasty, a connection that brought much fame and fortune to the house of Fugger.

But it was Jakob, the youngest son, born in 1459, that brought the greatest wealth and fame to the Lily Fuggers. Jakob became known as "Fugger the Rich." He expanded the family business to include the East Indies spice trade as well as wool, silk and linen into almost every part of Europe. Jakob later held a virtual monopoly in the mining and trading of silver, copper and mercury and also financed the election of Maximillian's grandson, Charles V, to the throne of the Holy Roman Empire in 1519.

Since Jakob the Rich had no sons, the family line continued through his nephew, Anton (1493-1560). Anton was made a Count and given the right of coining money. In those days, the Fugger bond was considered the most stable currency in all of Europe.

Eventually, the Fugger family revolutionized European commerce by introducing capitalist economic concepts and expanding international trade with their fleet of merchant ships. It was the Fuggers who invented the "check" to ease the flow of funds in their financial empire. Also, the newsletter they sent out on their ships, to inform their customers about world conditions was the forerunner of the modern newspaper.

Jakob the Rich, acting in the name of his brothers, Ulrich and George, had established a charitable fund to create the first welfare housing project in the western world. Known as the Fuggerei, it was to provide homes for Augsburg's needy Catholic citizens. The rent was only one rhenish guilder per year plus a daily prayer for the Fugger family. The Fuggerei has remained until the present day, with Prince Hubertus Fugger being one of the family descendents entrusted with guiding its destiny. Like his ancestors, Prince Fugger is also an astute businessman with many humanitarian concerns and aesthetic interests. In addition to keeping up the Fuggerei and managing the family estate and the Fugger Bank of Augsburg, he has expanded his business interests into the United States. He has now proven to have a keen interest and appreciation for America's history and culture. And although Prince Fugger is frequently addressed in Germany as "Your Serene Highness," he dislikes the distance that distinctions of class and title put between people. He is quick to tell his friends to call him Hubertus or even "Hubie."

Prince Fugger and his wife, Alexandra, have been blessed with five beautiful children, Franziska, Leopold, Alexander, Anastasia and Nickolus.

Appendix C

THE AUTHOR

A PERSONAL CONCEPT

When Godfrey Barnsley moved his family from Savannah to the Georgia up country in 1841, some of my ancestors were already settled in the area. Two of my great-grandfathers, Peyton Morrow and Wesley Sutton, became neighboring landowners to Barnsley, and later joined forces with him in opening up new roads through the Indian wilderness. The friendship that developed between them seemed to continue through the generations, for it was only a few years later, that Peyton Morrow began assisting Barnsley in developing his lands. In 1859, Peyton's daughter, Elizabeth, was born at Barnsley Gardens, and when she married my great-grandfather, Charles Callaway Sutton, in 1882, the ceremony took place in Godfrey's beautiful gardens. By the turn of the 20th Century, my grandfather, Emmanuel Sutton, worked for the chemist, B.F.A. Saylor. During the early 1900's, a great uncle, Carter Johnson, worked there as a horticulturist and farmer and began rearing his family at Barnsley Gardens. In 1935, after the final conflict between the Saylor brothers, some members of my family were among the first summoned to the aid of Mrs. Addie

Saylor. In 1945, my father purchased a portion of my grandparents' homestead, two miles from the Barnsley estate, and we frequently visited the families at Barnsley Gardens.

When I came into the world, I was named Philip Gregory Coker, being the eldest son of Sybil Sutton and Sherman Henry Coker. In the years to come, while working for an entertainment company, I would become known as Clent Coker. I was still only a toddler when my family first took me to visit Godfrey Barnsley's Woodlands in 1939. But I do vaguely remember sometime later, sitting in the parlor with Mrs. Addie Saylor and my great-grandmother, listening to the strange things they would talk about. I can also barely recall the Barnsley foreclosure auction of 1942, for I was there with my family, amidst the crowds and all the colorful heirlooms strewn over the grounds. But of course, more vivid in my mind were the hundreds of visits to Barnsley Gardens in the years thereafter. Probably the most treasured of my memories, however, go back to those cold winter nights sitting by the fireside with my great grandmother and my grandparents, listening to their tales of the Barnsleys that so intrigued me as a child. And then when I would lay down to sleep, I would often dream of the old Barnsley place and each of the characters in the stories they had told. I also remember when I was a bit older, traveling with my family over the main road through the "Woodlands," and the chill of excitement that came over me each time we passed Godfrey Barnsley's prominent hill.

One day in passing, I heard my great-grandmother remark:

"Poor Mr. Barnsley, lost so much to that ole war...just didn't care to live here any more, he died away down in New Orleans."

Yet I wanted to know why, but before she could answer I

heard my mother say:

> *"Well, I'm sure that dear Ms. Addie never got over that awful ordeal of Preston killing Harry. But we loved them both...it's such a shame things turned out that way..."*

But I became even more inquisitive, 'Why, Mother? Why did things turn out that way?'

Then suddenly I heard my father say:

> *"Oh, never mind son, it's nothing for children to be talking about, so just let it be."*

But in my mind, I couldn't just let it be. Even during those childhood years, I knew there was something different and very special about this family...this place!

As time progressed, my father would sometimes stop at the gardens to visit with Mr. Hubbard, the caretaker, and each time I would slip away, climbing the hill to the old Barnsley Manor, where I somehow felt a strong desire to be. And I am sure it was due to those Barnsley stories and dreams from my earlier childhood that I strangely felt I had been there many times before, and that, somehow, I was living part of its past.

However, as my visits continued, I began to realize something at Barnsley Gardens was still a bit unsettled. Some of the haunting legends that had long overshadowed the place were still not clear, thus leaving many of my questions still unanswered. As the days passed, I became filled with a burning desire to begin digging up all the pieces, remove the hidden skeletons, and gather all the facts in order to separate the truth from the many myths. It soon became a driving obsession that would lead me on a thirty-year journey, searching through the dusty trails of Barnsley history.

My journey began when I was still a boy walking the full country mile to visit the retired "Woodlands" overseer, Mr. George Sherman and his daughter Bertie Hanks, who certainly had their own Barnsley stories to tell. Each piece of Barnsley history they related, I carefully wrote down.

By 1952, my father had sold our small farm and we moved to another state almost a thousand miles away. Although I became involved with other interests, I would still often dream about the old Barnsley place. Then I would return to spend my summers at my grandfather's homestead, and of course, slipped off to visit Godfrey Barnsley's Woodlands almost every day. It was there I began searching for every piece of Barnsley history I could possibly find in the old buildings, junk filled barns, and the old abandoned cottage where many of Barnsley's papers had been stored since his death in 1873. Although many of his business papers had been distributed between three major universities (of which I would later research), there were still hundreds of fragments lying about that I carefully examined, piece by piece.

It was while visiting our family homestead, in the summer of 1954, that I would make an overwhelming discovery. I suddenly remembered that in my grandfather's house was a large roll top desk that had belonged to Godfrey Barnsley. It had been resting there since 1942, and of course while growing up, had become quite common place in the house and I had actually given it little attention. But now, as I was older, I could more fully appreciate its historical significance, and for some reason, felt a sudden urge to explore the old desk. Right away, I found in one of the upper compartments, a list of the Barnsley collections that had been sold at the 1942 foreclosure auction. Then while carefully crawling through the lower portion of the huge fixture, I discovered a large secret compartment, that would soon reveal great treasures.

Once I had pried open the door, much to my delight,

hundreds of well-concealed Barnsley papers fell directly into my hands. I naturally felt a great accomplishment, as I began sifting through four generations of family documents, photos, and old love letters from the Barnsley's past. I had thus established my first personal collection of original Barnsley papers that would continue for many years to come.

By conversing with elder members of my mother's family and searching through old letters I had found, I was able to compile a list of many of the former residents and servants of Woodlands who were still living in Northwest Georgia in the early 1950's. Since I was eager to interview them about their earlier lives at Woodlands, I soon had my friends and relatives take me to visit their homes. I would eventually find many of them in their seventies and eighties, and one lady at the age of 102. A short time later, when I was old enough to drive an automobile, I began taking many of them back to Woodlands, to walk them over the grounds, jog their memories and get their stories. Oh what beautiful treasures I had found! Many outstanding interviews were taken and filed away for future research.

During those days, I decided it would also be interesting to visit with some of the older merchants of the area who remembered doing business with the Barnsleys and Saylors. I would eventually interview many of them:

Down at the Hall's Station Junction, about three miles from Woodlands, Jess Taylor had, for many years, operated the general store, and so had his father before him. The Taylors soon furnished me a wealth of first hand information about their own dealings with the Barnsleys and Saylors. I also discovered that Taylors store was the most popular business spot on the twelve-mile stretch between Adairsville and Kingston, where local farmers and senior citizens regularly gathered to do their trading, or just sit around the old pot bellied heater and talk. So I began to spend much of my time at Taylor's store where I was able to interview many of the old timers who had spent their entire lives surrounding Barnsley Gardens. Through interviews and research I began to learn much of the interesting history surrounding those families, and began to visit some of their old homesteads. Many of those residents were still living in the same structures that had been standing since the War Between the States.

The Western & Atlantic Railroad route between Hall's Mill and Kingston was still dotted with naked chimneys and other ruins, that were authentic remnants from General W.T. Sherman's Atlanta campaign, back in the summer of 1864. The entire area surrounding Godfrey Barnsley's Woodlands, was indeed overflowing with rich history. It seemed as though time had passed it by and very little had changed along the old route since the mid-nineteenth century.

I could see, however, that many of them were in dire need of repair and if not protected, would soon vanish. As time passed, I began meeting with some of the owners of the properties and local businessmen, encouraging them to invest in the preservation of such a historic route. But unfortunately, my enthusiasm to save the local history was not always well accepted. While some agreed that such preservation was important, and did in fact support my interest, many others were not at all interested. To them, it was a foolish pursuit, too expensive, and a mere waste of time.

One day when I was discussing the local history with a lady in the back of Taylor's store, I overheard a customer say to Jess Taylor:

> *"Well, I see that boy's back again... aggravating folks about this old history stuff,.... he's always living in the past... just can't figure 'em out!"*

Needless to say, I was a bit embarrassed, and soon eased

out the door to sit on the wooden bench out front. But when the fellow had paid for his tobacco and left, Jess came out, patted me on the back and said:

> *"It's alright, son, some folks just don't understand or appreciate our history. But you know what you're doing and that's what counts, so keep right on with your work!"*

Well at least Jess was encouraging, and so I did as he said. I kept right on working!

While conducting one of the interviews, I had learned that Alice Butler Howard, a local teacher and historian, had also done some research on Barnsley's cotton business. She had acquired some of Godfrey's shipping ledgers along with a frock coat he had purchased in the 1850's. I soon began visiting Mrs. Howard's home, where she allowed me to study the ledgers. Thirty-five years later, I would receive the coat from an associate, Dan Biggers, and place it in the Barnsley Museum.

When I was first out of high school in 1955, my Barnsley research slowed down considerably, since I had found it necessary to take on various jobs, assisting my father with the support of the family. But I would still return during the summers, interviewing and researching on a part-time basis, and still dreaming that one day Barnsley Gardens would be discovered and restored.

During the 1950's, when I was still in my teens, I began to feel a strong urge to recapture the original Barnsley artifacts sold at the foreclosure auction in 1942. While growing up, I had kept notes of most of the major heirlooms, paintings and old photographs, and was acquainted with many of the individuals who had purchased them. But it would prove to be a lifetime project keeping track of the pieces, as they eventually became scattered through several generations of the families who owned them. However, as time progressed, I was able to purchase quite an extensive collection that would, many years later, be placed in the Barnsley Museum. I would also eventually receive other Barnsley relics that would be placed on loan to the museum.

Beginning in the late 1950's, I frequently traveled to Savannah, to visit the Georgia Historical Society and other archives, in order to research the "cotton" business of Savannah, in reference to Godfrey Barnsley and his father-in-law, William Scarborough II. It was there, I would later meet the Savannah Historian, Raymond Davis, who furnished me some additional photos, and papers on the William Scarborough family. It was also during those days that I began reviewing the portion of Barnsley papers that had been placed in four major universities by earlier members of the Barnsley family. And many years later, I would gather some information pertaining to the early cotton business of Georgia, from a dissertation prepared by Dr. Nelson Hoffman in 1964.

By the early 1960's, I was well pleased to discover that over ninety percent of the personal interviews conducted through the years, matched well with the documentation I had gathered, thus separating the facts from the many fables that had long overshadowed Barnsley Gardens.

Finally, one of the most valuable aspects of my research came from my correspondence with the Barnsley descendants throughout the United States and three foreign countries. I had already found at Woodlands and in the old Barnsley desk, some of the important records of Dr. George Barnsley, and his brother, Lucien, describing the locations of their families in Brazil and South America. As the correspondence progressed, I became closely associated with many of the descendants, who furnished me additional records and papers, and was warmly accepted, as the Barnsley Historian.

I would also collect some documents and photographs

pertaining to Barnsley's early life from his distant relatives in England and Australia.

Most of the documentation on the Saylor family however, was collected from a number of local sources, letters from relatives, and from Preston Saylor himself who had been released from prison in 1943, and was living near Atlanta, Georgia.

The first time I saw Preston "K.O. Dugan" Saylor was when I first visited his home in 1957. Although I had already gathered a great deal of information surrounding his life, I was still eager to meet this giant of a man who was somewhat of a legend in his own time. But K.O. Dugan, who had experienced a series of trials and tribulations in his life, seemed to possess a distrustful or paranoid characteristic, and was not an easy man to get to know. However, when he learned that I was the grandson of Emanuel Sutton, a friend and neighbor he had highly respected in the old days, I was immediately welcomed into his home. As my visits continued, K.O. Dugan finally began to open up, telling me the heart-wrenching story of his life while growing up at Woodlands.

As time passed, I cross-examined each one of his stories with the documentation and numerous interviews I had collected on his life. I soon came to the conclusion that K.O. Dugan was truly a man from the old school who had seemed to inherit many of the strong principles of his great-grandfather, Godfrey Barnsley; "right was right, wrong was wrong, a deal was a deal, and a man should live by his deals." I finally discovered that beneath that strong and battered hulk of a man could also be found a man of fairness and gentleness, although accompanied by many pains and fears that were repercussive of his younger days.

I would always remember the many enlightening visits to the home of K.O. Dugan Saylor. The last time I would see him would be at his bedside the night before his death in 1986.

In 1960, after working almost a year in the state of Michigan, I returned to North Georgia, and once again to researching and collecting artifacts on the Barnsleys. It was in 1961, that I met and married Laura Harris of Cassville, Georgia. Although history had not been one of her favorite subjects, she would sometimes accompany me on my research travels. *"In the years to come she would often tell our friends that we had spent our honeymoon trip to Savannah, trampling through old cemeteries to search out the Barnsley kin."* We were eventually blessed with six daughters and two sons, and I became involved with various businesses to support the family. Since I was from a family with a heavy musical background, and had a deep appreciation for music, I later became employed by a recording and publishing company in Nashville, Tennessee as a promoter, song writer and finally a recording artist. But it was an occupation that required much time away from home, and the dream of producing a story on the Barnsleys was put aside.

It was in the mid-1980's that I fully decided it was time to compile my years of research and interviews into a manuscript for a book. Since I had also dreamed of the story being turned into a motion picture, an associate soon introduced me to a retired film director who immediately became fascinated with my material, and suggested I write it into a screen script for a television mini-series. I therefore established a corporation that would legally own and control the project and joined forces with him to direct me in writing the screenplays. The project would continue on a part-time basis, for several years to come.

By this time however, I had given up all hope in Barnsley Gardens at Woodlands ever being preserved and decided that I never again wanted to view the grand old estate that was so rapidly fading into oblivion. Then came the year 1988, when Prince Fugger purchased the property, and I of course pleaded with him to save it.

Once he had made the decision to restore the gardens, I

was requested to be the resident historian, directing the Barnsley excavations, and later to establish the museum that I had long envisioned. Needless to say, I was suddenly filled with a new surge of energy and became heavily involved with the clean up and restoration project. The completion of the Barnsley story was again laid aside.

It was in the mid-1990's when the gardens had been opened to the public that I returned to writing a novel, and completing a screenplay on the Barnsleys. But once again, I would be forced to postpone the project. This time, due to a natural disaster.

On Sunday, March 27, 1994, I was quickly summoned to the Gardens to investigate a violent storm raging through the area that posed a threat to our guests visiting the grounds. After arriving, I was relieved to find that no one was injured, and the gardens had only received minor damage. When it seemed the storm had passed over, I returned to my own home, a few miles away, only to find it had been demolished by the same tornado, and worst of all, a dear neighbor had been killed in the storm. It proved to be a most devastating experience that will forever remain in our memories. Now, I could fully sympathize with the Barnsleys, who had suffered the same sorrow and effects from the storm that struck Godfrey's manor in 1906.

As family and friends gathered in to aid us with the disaster, it was discovered that many of my Barnsley papers, along with a final work copy of the screen script had received heavy water damage, and some had completely disappeared. For days thereafter, bits and pieces of my papers were found for miles away.

While spending the next two years rebuilding both physically and mentally from that catastrophe, I naturally suffered from fatigue and had little strength to return to the Barnsley story. But there was still no intention of giving up and I soon drew a second wind.

It was in 1998 that I decided it was time to, at least, compile this historical narrative and to complete one of the screenplays ready for presentation. This work would finally become a reality during the last few months of the 20th Century. A novel and another screenplay is still in the works.

It was also in 1999, that Prince Fugger proudly opened the new Barnsley Inn and Golf resort that would prove to be a wonderful way of extending Godfrey Barnsley's dream into the new millennium.

Although it has been a long and laborious journey searching through the many facets of the colorful Barnsley history, it has certainly proved to be a labor of love.

If I had it to do over, I'm sure I would do it all over again.

The Author

Clent Coker
Barnsley Author and Historian

AUTHORS ACKNOWLEDGMENTS

During the many years of research, conducting personal interviews, and collecting Barnsley artifacts, there were literally hundreds of people who contributed to my work. Many of them provided firsthand accounts that could not have been obtained from any other source, while others might have only furnished some small document or bits and pieces of information. Although each and every one was important to me, it would be impossible to note every person who assisted in some way. I do however, wish to acknowledge some of those special contributors who will forever remain in my memory.

First, I must mention that it all started during my childhood from the colorful Barnsley stories told by three generations of my family before me. It was the stories of my great-grandmother, Elizabeth Morrow Sutton, and my grandparents, Emanuel and Minnie Sutton, along with my great aunts, Louella Johnson, and Minnie Burley that first inspired me to search out the Barnsley history.

As time passed, I had the opportunity to interview many of the older residents of the area, who were truly a living part of the Barnsley History:

First there was George Sherman, the former Barnsley overseer, and his daughter, Bertie Hanks, who provided a great wealth of information. Also, many firsthand accounts were provided by Emma Pritchett, Fanny Colston, Molly Curtis, Mary Milsap, J.D. Green, Bessie Green, Nanny Waters, Simon Crowder, Clinton Culberson, Lollie Murphy, the Ned Phinnizy family, and Rose Phinnizy, John Conway, Ora Conway, Walter Lanham, Newt Freeman, George Freeman, the Dr. Burton family of Kingston, Jess Taylor, Cobb Green, Mary Kerr Lockridge, Earl and Ila McStotts, Arvil McStotts, Emily Jones

Harris, Dan Bowdoin, George Adams, Mrs. Claude Smith, Francis Sherman Blalock, Ralph Sherman, George Sherman, Jr., and Rex Sherman. Some of these also provided historic photos, letters and other small artifacts.

I will, of course, always be grateful for the many years of correspondence and interviews conducted with three generations of the Barnsley descendents. Among them were the families of Dr. George S. Barnsley, and Lucien Barnsley of Brazil, including the Holland and Grizzle families of California, and Hans Godfrey Barnsley Scheuenstuhl of Florida, the Allan Barnsley family of England, Jonathan Barnsley of Australia, Hoyt and Angela Scarborough, and Dr. Paulo Pessoa of Brazil. Then there was James Preston Saylor, of Atlanta, and Clarence Simms, and Bill Saylor of Seattle Washington.

From these sources, an extensive collection of Barnsley papers, letters, paintings and photographs were collected down through the years. Among them were numerous memoirs, letters and receipts of Godfrey and Julia Barnsley; the papers of Dr. George Barnsley including the family register, letters, copies of his Civil War diary, drawings, medical records, poems, and legal documents; letters, photos and documents of Lucien Barnsley; some letters and documents of Harold Barnsley, and Anna Gilmour Barnsley; early Barnsley family records from Great Britain, furnished by Allan, Michael, and Jonathan Barnsley; record books and treasured keepsakes of Captain James P. Baltzelle; letters, business papers and correspondence of the Baron Charles H. Von Schwartz; letters of correspondence of Julia Baltzelle Von Schwartz; a library of books, records, legal documents and photos of the chemist, B.F.A. Saylor; a collection of letters, photographs, legal documents, books and school records of Preston, Harry and Julia Saylor; the papers, photos and correspondence of Addie Saylor, Clarence Simms and Bill Saylor; letters, photos and memoirs of the Barnsley family servant, 'Uncle' Ned Phinnizy; letters of C.W. Howard in correspondence to the Barnsleys, and the collection of Barnsley papers and photographs owned by my grandfather, Emanuel Sutton.

In addition to this, some information and materials were gathered from the following sources:

- Early historians, Robert White and Joseph B. Mahan,

- the Alice B. Howard Collection of Barnsley letters,

- Lucy Conyus (Bartow County History 1932),

- the Raymond Davis Collection of Scarborough papers and photos,

- a partial collection of Wilbur Kurtz papers (Atlanta History Center),

- the Civil War records of Joe Tillman,

- the Civil War diary of Joseph Bogle,

- records of Barnsley's early cotton business in Georgia, from a dissertation prepared by Nelson Hoffman in 1964,

- the Georgia State Historical Society,

- some copies of letters and documents placed in the University of Georgia Library; the Robert W. Woodruff Library, Emory University, Duke University, and the University of North Carolina, by Barnsley family descendents.